CW00403358

Mary Magdalene's Great Passage

Journey into the New Earth

Published by Libraries of Light Media & Publishing
Libraries of Light is a trade name of Mary Magdalene's School
www.marymagdaleneschool.com

First edition 2022

Mary Magdalene's Great Passage
Journey into the New Earth

ISBN 978-90-9035467-5

Copyright © 2022
Libraries of Light Media & Publishing – Mary Magdalene's School

All rights reserved. No part of this book may be reproduced in any form or by any means,
electronic or mechanical, including photocopying, recording, or by any information storage
and retrieval system, without the prior written permission of the publisher.

Original content from Mary Magdalene's Great Passage online gathering:
Petra M. Brussen and Anna Vanickova

Scribe: Katherine Newburgh, PhD

Light Code Designs: Rosa-Maria Marquez

Book Design: Albertine Dijkema – A10design

Overall Publishing Support: Elise de Bres – Boekcoach.nl

Photograph on cover is the statue of Mary Magdalene in
the Basilique Sainte Marie Madeleine de Vézelay

KEY WORDS: 1. Mysticism 2. Spirituality 3. Meditation 4. Creation
5. New Earth 6. Gnostic Teachings 7. Body, Mind and Spirit 8. Sovereignty
9. Metaphysics 10. Enlightenment 11. Healing 12. Parapsychology

Mary Magdalene's Great Passage

Journey into the New Earth

©2022

Petra M. Brussen *&* Anna Vanickova

Mary Magdalene's School

scribed by **Katherine Newburgh**

Libraries of Light
Media *&* Publishing

Table of Contents

Live Transmissions

These meditations originated in Mary Magdalene's Great Passage online gathering. They have been transcribed for this book, with a few modifications. The New Earth is a deeply sensory place, bringing you into harmony with the wisdom of your whole body. Therefore, we offer the meditations also as they were given to the world – as spoken live transmissions. In listening to them you receive light codes through intonation, through cadence, through the transmitted universal voice of love.

While we offer short teachings before each meditation, you may be called to skip the teachings altogether and dive straight into the heart-journey that each meditation provides. Please feel free to do this!

The live series of meditations from the original online gathering can be ordered at: https://marymagdaleneschool.com/meditations/

Meditations of Mary Magdalene's School

The meditations from Mary Magdalene's School are guided transmissions from the field of the One Heart. We ask you to treat these transmissions with honour and respect. If you feel called to use these meditations outside the private domain (e.g. in group meditations or circles) you are FREE to use them by giving credit to Mary Magdalene's School. In so doing, you honour the original guidance and the Light Beings involved in this sacred work. We ask you to respect these guidelines as part of the copyright of these texts. If you wish to use them in any other way, please contact us at info@marymagdaleneschool.com.

Translations

Some of the live meditations of Mary Magdalene's School are translated, or are currently being translated, into other languages.

Please check our website for the latest translations: www.marymagdaleneschool.com.

No part of this book may be reproduced in any form or by any means, electronic or mechanical, including photocopying, recording, or by any information storage and retrieval system, without the prior written permission of the publisher.

We thank you for your understanding.

Mary Magdalene's School

⸕ We advise that people who have mental illness – who have undergone psychiatric care or other serious mental care – should NOT use these tools. This material requires us to be deeply anchored in the material world.

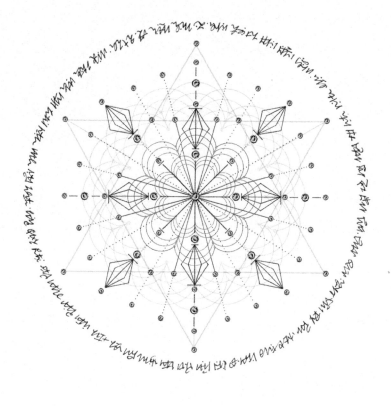

This book is dedicated to those
who have carried the light throughout the ages.

Preface

by Anna & Petra

Dear One,

We welcome you from the depth of our hearts to this shared sacred space! We are so grateful that our paths have crossed again, after what seems to be eons of time, to recapture the essence of our beings together! This is one of the greatest adventures a soul can live, and it is beyond anything we could have ever dreamed! We feel so very blessed to be able to live this experience with you.

Mary Magdalene's Great Passage is a passage of cosmic proportions for each and every human on earth at this time. Each and every one will go through this portal to the New Earth, by moving into the Sacred Heart and igniting the Chariot of Fire, the shining conveyance of truth within. And each and every one will do this in his or her own, magical, unique way, yet the big picture remains the same for us all. We will all find ourselves, at a certain moment or another, living life in a completely different way than we did in the old earth, united, joyful and in deep inner peace!

We will see that the master resides within our hearts and that the voice within is the only true one to support a beautiful, mysterious, rich and abundant life journey. It is the voice within that is the guiding force for the new story to emerge, and it is birthed with amazement and awe in a field of deep trust and unconditional love. What will emerge from this portal is a civilization rooted in the universal heart intelligence, fully honouring and abiding by the universal laws of nature.

We have no greater wish than to see this civilization of peace, harmony, and joy blossom on Gaia! We have waited patiently for so long, and we are thrilled beyond measure that we are now seeing the genesis of this new creation emerge. We have looked over the rainbow, and we have become the rainbow. And with that as our new starting point, let the magic begin!

Mary Magdalene's School

It was in 2020 that we were invited by Mary Magdalene to co-create a modern day mystery school in her name. Little did we know that it would result in one of the greatest gifts in our lives – to be of service to the creation of the New Earth under her guidance. Our whole-hearted YES activated a YES from many of our soul family around the globe. A deep knowing rose that we are all the awaited ones – we are all the ones with the gifts and the tools to move safely through the time of transition. We are all the ones who have incarnated on earth to help re-birth humanity into a community of the One Heart.

We perceive Mary Magdalene as a being who is all-encompassing. She is whole and holy. She knows all realms on earth and in the cosmos. She knows the ALL. And from that universal wholeness, she guides us in that ALL, in that wholeness, as the overlighting guide of our modern day mystery school.

In her presence, we were guided to create the global portal of the Great Passage and during the entire process, she tirelessly aligned us with the highest divine potential of the journey. We received the content of the Great Passage in many forms – through dreams, transmissions, images, words, metaphors, geometries, light codes, knowingness and remembrance.

Sometimes she spoke to us, and at other times she appeared as a physical embodiment in the subtle realms, as a friend and sister. At other moments, she moved into our bodies, unifying at a cellular level her consciousness with ours. Yet on other occasions, we would speak and realize we were using her words, or we would write her thoughts that were downloaded into our field of consciousness.

We have been asked to pioneer human consciousness by stepping into her source of illumination and mystical power. This experience is life changing, because we are not working on the peripheral fringes of mysticism. We have entered a state of consciousness through which we engage directly with the quantum energy field, the source of the divine force that exists in the vortex and portals at the centre of the Light. The result of this is a merging of dimensions, an infinitely practical way of bringing real, tangible, concrete changes to the realm of form in which we live.

Mary Magdalene's School, as it is emerging, gives the individual a choice to choose Oneness in a manner that was not existent before, as the school itself is a new, living geometry of light. It arose from the universal field of the flower of life, as light fractals of a Magdalene creation that is forming a new consciousness for humanity. And we are instruments of this divine intention for the manifestation of a whole new energy system.

The vibration of this mystery school is a fertile womb. It is a Holy Grail. And we are the guardians of the purity of that which is given life through this womb of the Divine Feminine; we are guardians of this sacred gift. We walk this path of service in deep humility to the cosmic forces of nature.

Mary Magdalene's Great Passage Online Gathering

In Mary Magdalene's Great Passage online gathering, we rejoiced at collectively inhabiting the space of the One Heart. Mary Magdalene's guidance through the Great Passage was miraculous, surprising and full of grace, and those who participated felt this deeply. Her community gathered together from many countries, from many different traditions and from many realms. We were exposed to, and collaborated with, many Light Beings who gave guidance and direction, and shared their wisdom. We experienced a whole new way of being in the world, as planetary and galactic citizens remembering our place in creation. This was a true celebration of the magic of life!

One global online gathering led to another over a period of six months, as we were shown that the work we were doing collectively needed to go ever deeper and expand into ever widening realms of consciousness. The second gathering of this series was on the Twin Flame Oneness Consciousness, and the third was called the Coronation of the Sacred Masculine. All together, they created a Rainbow Bridge to the New World.

Together we celebrate the first book, which is also the first book emerging from Libraries of Light Media & Publishing. The Great Passage is intended as a guide for our soul family through this transition time, to support the process of purifying and uplifting our consciousness, connecting to the Sacred Space of the Heart, igniting the Light Body to access and inhabit our original multidimensional nature, leading to the use of our full human capacities. This process of remembering can sometimes feel like a labyrinth and it is very helpful to have a guiding light to know that we are held by Eternal Grace.

We are in a deep state of humility and gratitude as we co-create this book with Mary Magdalene's guidance. We are most honoured to share the teachings she finds important for humanity at this time. She is opening our consciousness to the records of the Libraries of Light so that they can be re-introduced into the world in a whole new way, aligned with the times in which we are living.

Our Scribe, Katherine Newburgh (Kate)

We have experienced countless miracles since we started Mary Magdalene's School. One of the greatest ones has been our encounter with Kate. When she appeared on the horizon, the word "scribe" flashed at us through her energetic-informational field, but it took a few months to understand what it was that Mary Magdalene was orchestrating! Kate arrived in Mary Magdalene's School through the wind of timelines, ready to honour her deep gift, and her vow to her own Great Passage. Her commitment to the process brought her to Vézelay, France, where we spent three months closely collaborating in a multi-layered, multidimensional manner, in a process of mutual and collective illumination.

In a space of reconstitution, we met each other deeply. We re-membered ancient vows of co-creation, and we re-membered the sanctity of the scribe. We pieced together age-old relationships, experiences, and skills, which were brought together at this time through divine guidance for this very special purpose. We were in awe at the manner in which Mary Magdalene brought together her team, from across the earth, fully committed to this sacred task of writing books from the Libraries of Light. Together we experienced the deep wonder of the divine creation mechanism, activated when we say YES to our sacred life path.

We are so deeply grateful for Kate's YES, for her profound commitment to her vow of service in this time of transition. We honour her as the scribe of this book. It is her mastery of alchemical writing, her ability to feel a book as a whole being before it is even started, and her deep love and respect for the sanctity of the book during the whole process, that allows these records to be presented in this completed form.

Judith Moore

Visionary, medium, and wisdom keeper, Judith is devoted to the Divine Order and has for decades been deeply engaged in bringing the Magdalene consciousness into the world. She is an elder who has opened the records of the God Ra, the Magdala Force, the Arc of the Covenant and many more. We feel a deep lineage to her work as these records continue to come into the human consciousness.

We have been very touched by the depth of illumination and mystical transmission that Judith has lovingly and generously provided us with about the role of revelation through Mary Magdalene's School. Her visions have been deeply supportive to our process and have helped us gain immense clarity about the scope and direction of the material that we are called to bring into the world.

Judith's presence in the creation phase of this book shone a light on the depth and significance of the writings. Her insights stem from her long-term work with the Magdalene force and her resonance with the material we have been asked to bring into the world. Judith's revelations give a deeper meaning than we could have imagined to the process we are undergoing. We are ever so grateful that she accepted to write a foreword, which we feel like a sacred baptism for this baby, this inaugural book of the Libraries of Light. It is blessed in a beautiful way with her imprint, her Christ vibration of Oneness.

And now, we most joyfully welcome you, reader, into this Passage through Mary Magdalene's Way of Love, the Way of the Feminine Christ.

Petra M. Brussen & Anna Vanickova

This book, touching down from the Libraries of Light,

Rings through Gaia like a tolling bell.

It vibrates with a resonance that enters your heart,

Lighting up the long-forgotten desires of your soul.

Foreword

Judith Moore

I was brought into Mary Magdalene's School when Anna, Petra, and Kate invited me to participate in the flow of the liquid light and the miraculous force that will go forth from this book. You said, "Sister, we welcome you into the mystery school, to be part of the sacred journey we are making to send this manuscript of light into the world." I am grateful to be a part of such a gift. I knew the only way I could write the foreword is from the spirit of the communion of our souls as Magdala Sisters. As we sat together in communion, I felt the message of the Magdala Source rise within me...

These sacred teachings have been protected by the Covenant of Light until the time of the awakening of the Divine Feminine. The vibration and the essence of Mary Magdalene must now be made accessible to more people than just those who understand the hidden mysteries.

The Great Passage brings the essence of the hidden mysteries and the vibration of the Magdala force into a form that touches peoples' hearts and awakens their spirits, to realize their divine connection with the Source of All Oneness. The teachings are the secrets of the Holy Grail.

Through this work, you are invited to make a journey of self-discovery and awakening. The teachings offer a practical way for daily devotions that awaken your connection to the Divine Mother within your heart and soul. Within these pages you are given sacred tools and techniques that are like the leavening of the bread of life. You have the ingredients, and now you must hold the sacred bread of life in your hands and work with it. You knead the bread, you pour your love into it and it rises with the leavening of the ancient mysteries, becoming warm within you.

You prepare a sacred feast that feeds your mind, body, spirit and soul for the Bread of Life so that you may offer your gifts to others.

It is the Eucharist of Life because it is mystical and in a very real way it is applicable to your ability to discover tools, awareness and techniques that enhance your life on this earth plane. These teachings enrich your spirit and give you a foundation for the expansion of your consciousness. The foundation is something solid to stand on as you go through your life journey.

You made a choice in your life that led you to open this book. When you opened this book, you chose to pick up these tools to build a new world of peace.

The most precious treasures of wisdom passed to humanity by the masters are both mystical and accessible. Hand people tools and they will build a new world of peace. And these are the tools, the gifts, of this book.

Every word in this book is infused with a vibration of the essence of Oneness from the source of the soul of Mary Magdalene. She has translated the mysteries into a form that, like bread, can be held in the hand, and that can be understood and used. This is the mysticism of the Magdala force, as a practical life journey that opens every single person as they open the book.

You are invited to say "YES! I can achieve mastery!" This is a pathway and it shines the light of the Way of Love for the souls of those who are called to open this book. It is a vital link connecting mysticism to practical skills and tools that awaken the spirit and bring the soul to the light.

Mary Magdalene called the authors to birth this gift to humanity from the heart of her immortal soul. She is present, she is with you. Open your heart as your read and you will feel her love.

Blessed be, so be it and so it is.

Judith Moore

Gratitudes

by Anna & Petra

We would like to thank the following people for supporting the creation of this book. Truly, without you, this work could not have been possible.

From the depth of hearts, we thank our husbands, David Jandejsek and Philip van der Linden, without whom non of this work would have been made possible. They make the container to hold not only this book, but indeed all the projects of Mary Magdalene's School. Antharion (Ton Steenvoorden) – your commitment beyond the veil is divine and eternal. Your bringing in of the Oneness Consciousness has deeply supported the process of our work and this book. Traveller, our crystal skull elder, shared his cosmic intelligence in unexpected ways, guiding us beyond the boundaries of our own perception.

Janneke Schmidt – our angel assistant and guiding light in the background of all our work – we deeply thank you for all your service, day in and day out.

Vera Holland and Anika Lewis, we thank you for your countless hours of transcriptions and positive presence. Henk Kruithof & brother (wishing to stay anonymous), we thank you for your great generosity of spirit. We would like to thank Noreen Berger for her unfailing angelic presence and her meticulous proof reading of the final manuscript.

Elise de Bres, you made our journey through the publishing world feel so easy with your warmth and expert guidance. Rosa-Maria Marquez, our collaboration was a great gift from the higher realms! Albertine Dijkema, we felt held and carried by you in your proficiency of book design. Rob Leenders, our consultations on the design of the visual were a beautiful support.

We want to express a heartfelt thank you to our focus group that read earlier versions of this book and gave very precious, thoughtful and heartfelt feedback. This was the essential compost needed to bring the book into its final form. Thank you Annie Waugh, Jouke Posma, Cindy Osborne, Nick de Zwart, Nicolas Perrin, Vera Holland, Henk Kruithof, Janneke Schmidt and Geraldine Harris.

We would like to thank the entire town of Asquins, France for holding our scribe as she transitioned into the frequency of Mary Magdalene in order to write this book. Special thanks especially to Lucy, Phil, Valerie, Stefan Noreen, and Clara for making her stay joyful and supported. A special thank you to Claude Clavel, from la Vieille Borde, for your generosity and support.

We would like to honour Drunvalo Melchizedek, who taught the world so much about the Sacred Space of the Heart and the Tiny Space of the Heart. We have greatly benefitted from his loving, generous and tireless teachings. We would also like to honour the anonymous masters who provided elements for The Temple of Divine Will and Love meditation.

This book is based on the original Mary Magdalene's Great Passage online gathering, in which over 15,000 people from 150 countries participated. Many people were fundamental to making this online gathering the success it was, and we want to thank you from the depth of our hearts: Naomi van Dorst, Angélique van Cleef, Janny Bijma, Yvonne Verhagen-Verlijsdonk, and Erik Verhagen.

We have been unconditionally supported by many people in our community, and we are extremely grateful that you are pillars of love and clarity when we need it! We wish to extend a heartfelt thank you to the Mary Magdalene's School community, to the Re-membership Group, because each and every one of you is so deeply committed to remembering and living Oneness Consciousness. You have gone through the process with us, you have shared your stories and inspired us, and you are the guiding lights of the New Earth. Last but not least, thank you Peter Olsson, Margaret Claire Jacobs, Annie Waugh, Dvora Pearlman, Ton van der Kroon, Anne Wislez, Monique Willemsen and

Marcel Nijenhuis. Your unconditional love has held us throughout the journey.

Petra M. Brussen & Anna Vanickova

Feel the ground under your feet,

Hold smooth stones in your hand,

Breathe into your body

The charged freshness of dawn,

Listen to the birds, the wind, the rain,

Singing your divinity back to you.

Part 1

Introduction

Welcome.

Your presence has been eagerly anticipated for some time now. Lifetimes, in fact. You may see in front of you an open door. On the other side shines a light so bright that it drowns out shape and form. You stand here on the threshold, looking in.

You have been traveling toward this moment for as long as you can remember. Each step you've taken in this life – and in lifetimes past – has led you here. Let your shoulders release their tension. Unclasp your hands and open your fingers. Breathe deeply into your own indwelling stillness. It's time now to come home.

Welcome Traveller. Welcome Home.

You are holding in your hands no ordinary book. This book seems to have borders to it. You can feel the two covers, run your fingers along the edges, and count the pages. But this book is, in fact, infinite. The words running through this book live as golden text on a velvet ribbon. It stretches out as the Uroboros in an unending loop of creation. As you follow the ribbon around and around, you will discover a living world that exists beneath the words.

This is the world of spirit. It reveals itself in the echoing wisdom of shape and sound, in and between the glyphs we call consonants, we call vowels. This subterranean living world breathes through the silence, the stillness that surrounds you as you read. This world exists in the heart of you, where the journey of your soul has been faithfully recorded throughout the ages. This book in your hands is, quite literally, a living document, as it will be your own consciousness that brings it to life. The life you breathe into it, however, is as unique as your thumbprint, as irreplaceable as the story of your soul.

As you read, you may feel the unlocking of something deep within you, a releasing of memory that at a certain point was shut down. Listen to this unlocking; watch these inner doors swing open. Behind them are gifts of knowledge that you have held all along. They point you unerringly toward the purpose of your existence. You are here for a reason, after all, and your body and heart hold within them a bone-deep knowledge of that reason.

As you open this book you also open a door to another world. It is time now to cross the threshold. In this you are facing a death of sorts, a letting go, a leaving behind of what you once thought to be true. You have willingly outgrown those old thoughts, and you can allow them now to pass away. Once you do, there will be no going back to the person you once were. The old self and the new cannot exist in the same place at the same time because they live in two separate worlds. Therefore, you must choose. But if you are here, you are not actually the chooser, but the chosen. This moment and this choice have already been written into the text of your life. You would not be standing here otherwise.

You do not need to worry that you will be traveling through this new world alone. While your own journey is unique, there are many on the path with you. You will recognize them by the way they resonate with the song of your own Sacred Heart. We are constructed of sound, of vibrations and light frequencies, and the souls who strike chords with your own are your fellow pilgrims, toning forth harmonies of the New World that we are birthing into being. As you access the resonance of this book and align with it, these communities of light will magically appear around you where they seemed to not exist before.

As you turn inward to trust the voice of your own Higher Self, you will touch the essence of the divine mystery. This is where trust and faith are necessary. The journey through your wild inner terrain will bring you into contact with many guides from other realms of existence. If you are lost, you need only offer up a simple, heart-felt invocation through thought or word, and they will appear. Sometimes it takes a little time to sensitize your system to feeling them through the subtle realms. But these beings are faithful and ever-loving. Their highest intention is to help you uncover the deep truths of your heart's purpose. When you feel lost in the storm and clamour, when you cannot hear yourself through the noise of the world, they can clearly hear your inner voice. They will always steer you truly, into greater and greater awareness of your own Highest Self.

You may be drawn to one, two, or many of these guides. Trust that whomever magnetizes you has great teachings to offer. Like a honeybee that is drawn to flowers by currents unseen from the outside, you do not need to have any discernible order to your movements. Neither should you feel like you must force a relationship with any guide or teaching that does not resonate with you in the moment. All you need will be revealed to you at exactly the right time in exactly the right way.

This book offers to you the blueprint, the treasure map, the bones of your own personal mythology. It provides a framework, a pathway through which you can build your grandest, most perfect castle and manifest it in your current life. You are the hero of your own fairytale, and it just so happens that yours is a true story. Believe in the visions that arise as you read this book. They come from a deep source of life, wisdom, and knowing within you. Believe in the urgings, the longings, the truths that you un-cover. Believe it is all true, all available, and already written. Your imagination is so much more than what you have known so far. It's now time for you to experience the limitless creative power of your heart. It is time for you to see what you can create through the unending expanse of unconditional love that dwells within you.

The words of this book have

Slipped through the dimensions

To come to you now.

As you read, you inhale

The essence of their origin.

You recognize this fragrance.

Libraries of Light

Shining at the heart of the echoing realms of the unseen are vast Libraries of Light. All that has ever been known, all that has been written and spoken by the holy mechanism of the word dwells within these libraries. You stand at the vaulted doorway and see them spreading before you like a small city, glowing bright with the unmistakable knowledge of all that is.

Enter now. Allow yourself to wander the vast passageways, let your fingers run along the spines of endless rows of volumes. Large, small, rough, smooth, velvety, knobbly, the books shimmer, each one emitting its own, perfect, and unmistakable frequency. Each book glimmers with hidden secrets, beckoning you to touch, to sense, to absorb its radiance. All that has ever been known, all that will ever be known, is recorded here. You now freely walk these halls of infinite knowing. You now hold at your fingertips the knowledge of all that has ever been and all that will ever be.

Listen to the silky ribbon of your breath as you tread in awe through a vast silence, stepping in footfalls that echo through the realms of time. The floor beneath you has been worn smooth by the many beings that have traversed its length.

Unbidden, you find yourself walking down a shining corridor that emanates a diamond-blue light, at once soft and icy, inviting and ethereal. At the end of the corridor there is a wall. You walk to the end of this row and touch the wall. You have arrived at the beginning.

It dawns on you that this hall has never before been entered. As you stand gazing at the rows and rows of glowing books you realize that each of them has yet to be opened. No consciousness has yet shone its light upon their sacred words. Each book before you is a capsule of wisdom waiting to be unlocked by those ready to bring life to its pages. These books hold their secrets and tremble with anticipation at the touch of your awareness. With your breath you breathe life into their pages; with your consciousness you give them the wings they need to alight like a dove on earth.

This book, the one you hold now in your hands, is the first one in this row. The words of this book have slipped through the dimensions to come to you now. As you read you inhale the essence of their origin. You recognize this fragrance. It is somehow familiar to you. It smells of home and warmth; it smells of a place you have never left. The words woven here drop into your consciousness, blooming within you as the resurrection of a long-distant spring.

As you stand in this corridor of books, all around you wafts this fragrance of Source, waking up your senses and carrying you forward into the Eden of your being. Let the words of this book wash over you, evoking the diamond purity of your own Eternal Light. Let them beckon your soul to emerge from the darkness of the ages. Let them wake up in you an ancient wisdom, the one you know and have always known, which lives within you. This is your heartsong, your soul's unequivocal essence. It opens the invocation of your own Sacred Heart, waking, once and for all, the wisdom that sleeps within you.

The World Behind the Veil

This book offers to you eight crystal stepping-stones, each one taking you farther into the glimmering depths of your own unfathomable soul. These crystal stones, as you traverse them again and again, as you lay your feet upon their smooth, crystal surface, will bring you deeper and deeper into the truth of your Illumined Heart. Within you are etched the stories of ages. Within you rest, undiscovered, the diamonds of wisdom you have gathered carefully from lifetimes of walking these lands. The eight crystal stones lead you to the diamonds within, waiting patiently to be gathered in your hands like glittering dawn-salt from the sea.

The eight stones offer you a path to the Sacred Space of your Heart, from where the New Earth will be born. With each faithful step you will find, beneath your feet, a perfect encoded crystal transmitted directly from Source. We call these stones "meditations," but this single word cannot convey their power.

Each meditation in this book holds messages for you, but you must know now: these messages cannot be understood by your thinking mind. When you read, when you listen, let your mind rest from fear and worry. As the words wash over your body, listen as they activate truths from the pure, diamond centre of your being. These truths will rise to the surface to be bathed in the glow of your quiet and gentle heart, but they will vanish if exposed to the brash light of your thinking mind.

The memories of your soul are ready now to be unlocked. Your purpose, your role in the New Earth, is ready to be transmitted to you. As you listen, as you read, the hidden secrets of your soul's purpose, the ancient knowledge of your soul's mastery will open to you like lotus flowers, blooming from places you had never thought to look. For you this knowledge may take the form of feelings, emotions, visions, sensations, or sudden understandings that drop like pebbles into the still water of your consciousness.

Whatever the form of your revelations, trust in their ability to lead you past the swirling darkness of illusion and into the sunlit realm of your truth and purpose. These are ancient memories that transmit to your waking consciousness the forgotten powers of your soul. Once you are brushed with the light of your own grace, you will never again forget who you are.

Remember now. We take you back all those eons ago when you walked with freedom and naturalness into the etheric temples of the earth to learn the ancient secrets contained therein. In those days, the temples were material and visible to your physical eyes. They rested on the surface of the planet, raised by loving human hands directly on the potent power spots of Gaia's converging ley lines. Back then the whole earth was a place of worship, and the keepers of these temples lived in harmony, freely sharing wisdom and knowledge with each other.

These temples still exist, but they have been forgotten. They dwell behind the veil, behind the dark shroud of perception woven by the thinking mind. The keepers of these temples await your arrival with anticipation and joy. They long to meet you and show you once again their ways of ancient wisdom and magic. As you meet the keepers, you may discover a sense of familiarity, a homecoming. This is because your souls are known to each other from a time way back. These temples were once your sanctuaries, the whole earth your home. These keepers await your return so they can show you again the wisdom you once knew and the mastery that you carry. These keepers honour your courageous human journey, your choice to incarnate as a wayshower of light on the planet. They wait with anticipation to unite with you once again.

The eight crystal stones of these meditations lead you to these temples of light with ease and softness. As you journey, these meditations soothe the worry of your thinking mind like a cool hand placed on a heated brow. These meditations lift the veil, with reverence and gentleness, to reveal the magic waiting behind it. Indeed, there is a vast landscape living just on the other side of the surrender of your thinking mind. The magic beyond beckons you to the threshold of this world.

As you peer into this unknown and familiar world, the meditations guide you safely through the wondrous terrain of this unmapped landscape.

You may think these meditations are fantasy, and indeed, the world they reveal is one of magic and joy that we, in this realm, have long since relegated to the realm of fairytale. We assure you that these journeys are real. These places you visit in the Sacred Space of your Heart are real. The beings, guides, gifts, and all of the understandings that come with them, are real. As you witness places long forgotten by our current, busy world, the power of your faith invites you to believe in this realm of magic and wonder. Our belief heralds the merging of these worlds once again so we can live in harmony and union as one body on Gaia.

Once you are brushed with the light of your own grace,
You will never again forget who you are.

The Great Passage

As you peer across the swirling silver eddies of the vast river before you, you see on the far bank the faint outline of a glowing Being of light. This Being radiates bright, multi-coloured light. As you continue to gaze at its captivating beauty, you suddenly realize that all of the colours of Gaia radiate from her aura. This Being stands like the dawn on the unknown land of the far bank. You wonder about the vast, unknown terrain on which the Being stands.

This Being is you. This is the you that has claimed your Rainbow Light Body, your birthright as a human on this planet.

Eight meditations lie before you now, awaiting you in the pages of this book. Each meditation is a step on your path to reclaiming this Sacred Body of Light – the body of the New Earth. These meditations were brought forth in the weeks leading up to the potent time of earth's crossing into the New Earth: December 21, 2020. This was the moment that we stepped over the threshold into a New Age of Unity. These meditations guide us on this Great Passage into a new era.

Though that specific timeframe has passed, these meditations live on as precise transmissions of energy from that fertile Passage into the New Earth. They glow like seeds, each with its own unique Christed Light, perfect time-capsules holding the energy of our collective Passage. When you enter into these meditations, you are brought on your own journey of rebirth. Mary Magdalene, in her infinite grace, takes you by the hand and guides you safely through this Great Passage from separation into a reunion with yourself.

This book brings the New Earth to life in all of our senses. Sitting side by side on the newly-accessed shelf in the vast Libraries of Light, we bring it forward now as a tool for embodying the New Earth within us.

We come now to lightly brush over the body of this work: the eight crystal stones, the meditations that will wake up the power that lives within each of us.

The Opening Ceremony and First Meditation

With this ceremony you prepare to cross the great river in front of you. As you approach the riverbanks, allow yourself to be brought gently into the transformative field of your coming Passage. Let this meditation prepare you to step confidently onto the crystal stones that have been cast in a glittering, rainbow arc before you. Allow your body, mind, and soul to relax so you may receive the teachings of your heart. Let the guides and protectors from the earth and cosmic realms come to you with their love so you may know you walk in perfect safety and peace.

The Second Meditation

This second meditation brings you into the loving arms of the Divine Mother. Let her hold you so that all fear and doubt melt away. Feel her frequency anchoring within you so that you may offer it to others. She shows you her love so that you may always recognize it through the noise and clamour of this world. Rest in her arms and know that you are loved, unconditionally and without limit.

The Third Meditation

This third meditation beckons you into the first heart-dreaming journey of the Passage. Follow the guidance of your heart as it carries you to the shores of Lake Titicaca where you are welcomed to enter the Divine Temple of Illumination. Meet the Divine Feminine Council as they gather to oversee the healing and needs of our planet. Allow yourself to be connected to the hearts of your Divine Mother and Father so that they may bring you your birthright of diamonds and gold.

The Fourth Meditation

This fourth meditation leads you gently to accept the healing power of Divine Love. Let yourself be guided to use your voice and free will as an instrument for clearing, purification, and healing. Rest in the strong, capable hands of the Arcturian healers as they remove all energies that cause you pain and suffering. Let these energies fall away so that your soul's purpose can be revealed.

The Fifth Meditation

This fifth meditation bathes you in the unmistakable frequency of unconditional love. This is the frequency of the New Earth – the frequency you will be called to embody. Open and receive gold and rubies as they pour into your energy body through the sacred threefold flame.

The Sixth Meditation

This meditation leads you into the most sacred place in the whole universe. Let yourself enter the gates of your own Tiny Space of the Heart and be opened to the wonders of your own creative power. This is the centre of all creation, dwelling inside of you.

The Seventh Meditation

Wake up to the smells and excitement of the day before a big celebration. This meditation is a time of final preparation. Let yourself be swept up in the joy of final adjustments. Relax as your body, mind, and soul are opened to receive the blessing of your Rainbow Light Body – the body of the New Earth.

The Eighth Meditation and Closing Ceremony

The meditation leads you into the light of a new day. Celebrate, for you have arrived! Accept the birthright of your Holy Light Body. Emerge from this Passage into the light of the New Earth as a confident and free sovereign creator. Take your place as one who sets in motion healing, ascension and unity for all of humanity.

A Gathering of Souls

This book, touching down from the Libraries of Light, will ring through Gaia like a tolling bell. It vibrates with a resonance that enters your heart, lighting up the long-forgotten desires of your soul. Let these desires awaken within you now. Trust their power and clarity. Trust the unremitting voice that urges you onward. You can feel these heart desires shining like a treasure beneath the turbulent waters of this illusionary world. They beckon you into the depths of yourself.

This book calls you to live the deepest desires of your soul. As you follow the shining light of your heart's longing, you will recognize your fellow pilgrims journeying with you. They walk alongside of you with their ears and eyes turned inward, listening to that voice that none other can hear, following that light that none other can see. These are your brethren. Together you are wayshowers for the New Earth, and as you walk together, you realize this New Earth can only be realized in communion; it does not, cannot exist in the realm of separation. This book is a siren call of Eden, beckoning to you in a clear, sweet voice to come out of hiding.

This is the time of our prophesied reunion. We come together after being scattered by the flood – the cataclysm that fragmented us so long ago.

This book offers a journey of re-membering. It helps you locate the fragments of soul that you had hidden from yourself through the lifetimes. The fragments of your soul that were hidden are waiting in the oddest of places, with the strangest of people. They wait like shining jewels to be recovered, one by one, on your heroic human quest.

The Self we assemble in this process of re-membering will be illumined by a new wisdom, gained by our eons of traversing the darkness. As we piece together the fragments of our souls, we see the seams where we fit them together illumined in light. We see that these are not scars but shining rivers of molten gold, the result of alchemy rising from the seasons of darkness. These seams of the soul shine in glowing testimony to our resilience and strength, the endless and undaunted reality of the divine, creative power of humanity. Nothing is stronger than our light. With our love, we magnetize to us our scattered pieces and emerge, as we have always been, whole, perfect, and divine. The light within us takes shape as our own bodies, and we feel the whole of the universe twinkling through every cell, every atom, every breath of our being.

We are no longer concerned with what was. We are no longer interested in the forces of separation and darkness. We have shed the old world like a tough outer skin that no longer fits our shape. The world we came from begins to seem like a distant dream. We have alchemized it through the fabric of our being and have become captivated instead by our own radiance and vitality. We have lifted beyond and fallen deeply in love with our True Selves. No darkness can compete with the unending love we feel towards our whole, unbroken divinity. That darkness becomes but a whisper of things long past, a faint brush of memory that cannot hold our attention.

As we look around, we finally see each other. We come to understand that we are surrounded by old, old friends with whom we have been traveling for a long, long time. As I look into your eyes, I know you. I see the glint of recognition. I reach out to you from the shining chalice of my heart and feel your presence within me. I am no longer fooled by your disguise of flesh and bone. I am bathed in your radiance and as we behold each other I feel my own love reflected back to me, warm and comforting like fire in a hearth, like a perfect cup of tea passed simply and joyfully from one hand to another.

You will look up from the pages of these books and recognize the brothers and sisters of light gathered around you. Those with recognition shining in their eyes will be your sanctuary and your support as you learn to gaze with awe upon the infinity of your being and the wonder of this world.

It is ok to gather with those who reflect your own light. It is ok to hold your secrets and your wisdom close until such a time as they are ready to be revealed. It's ok to seek out those who are consciously walking the path with you to wholeness and unity. Let yourself be lifted into communities of light where your own heart's desires can be cherished, nourished, and held. Trust that nothing and no one is ever lost. Trust that tending to those desires, shining deep within you like jewels, is the greatest gift you can offer the world.

At this time, as we tend to our own inviolable shining, it is enough to know that all of those we meet are walking toward the light, even when it seems that they are stumbling in darkness. To judge the butterfly's journey by how quickly or how directly it reaches its destination would be to miss the beauty and grace of its flight, the way it flutters like joy on the unseen eddies of the wind, the way it declares its perfection with every unpredictable swoop and spiral of its being. Like the butterfly, we know transformation. We know the paths that carry us on the unseen swirling of a breeze. Only we can feel these forces that direct us. No other can define these eddies for us, nor can they fully understand or predict our own sacred journey to the light of our being. So we honour each other and our journeys, waiting with anticipation for the stories of wisdom that will crystalize from that which each of us have seen and heard. We trust that, just as our own individual being has come together in an ecstasy of reunion, everyone we meet holds a story that will illuminate the infinite shape of our collective being. Every journey and every story is vital to the wholeness of the New Earth. We know that someday, when our Passage is complete, we will gather around the fire and each of us will tell our tale of adventure and love and resilience and grace.

We shine, then, walking the earth in our own illuminated wisdom and honouring the light, the darkness, the words, and the choices of all whom we meet. We trust the divine hand that is guiding us all toward our own inevitable blossoming.

Our heart is the voice that will lead us,
Our soul the light that shows the way.

Let yourself be lifted into the communities of light

Where you own heart's desires can be

Cherished, nourished and held.

Preparing for
the Great Passage

Listening to the Body

As you read, allow the encodings in this language of light wash over you. Perhaps these words are nourishing something deep within your soul that you didn't know was hungry. Perhaps, though strange and different, you feel as though the most familiar part of you is finally being brought to the surface to be recognized.

Your body will experience the shifts of this Passage at a cellular, molecular, and indeed at an atomic level. You can rest assured that your body is ready for these shifts and can guide you to all that it needs. On our spiritual paths, we may dwell in those higher realms beyond the physical. However, our soul is formless, and our body is the great gift we receive for our human experience. This Passage is an invitation to let your body integrate the highest frequencies of light. Listen to the voice of your body. Trust it. The body is of this earth and knows the deepest secrets of creation. Allow your body's needs and wants to guide you through this Passage. It will reveal to you its secrets as a magical, alchemical creation.

The body may ask for things that are new to you. It may ask for shifts in nourishment, lifestyle, movement, and rituals. Trust its voice. Trust that it will guide you to the resources, people, and practices that will allow you to embody your highest frequencies of light.

Our bodies are of the earth and they yearn to be in harmony with her. As we return to a natural relationship with the earth through this Passage, prepare to learn from her rhythms, through your body sensations. Most likely, you will be guided to slow down in your life and make time to commune with the infinite wisdom of nature. If at any point you feel overwhelmed, you can turn to Gaia as your Divine Mother and guide. Feel the ground under your feet, hold smooth stones in your hand, breathe into your body the charged freshness of dawn, listen to the birds, the wind, and the rain singing your divinity back to you. Let yourself tune into Gaia as your loving, Divine Mother, and she will guide your body into its natural resonance.

Listening to the Higher Self

This book offers a pathway, again and again, into the Temple of Your Heart, showing you the way back to your own sovereignty: that time when you claim the voice of your heart as your highest and only guide. This Passage will offer space and time to practice listening to the needs and direction of your heart. At all times, allow yourself to take what resonates and leave what doesn't. You can remain open to new experiences while also letting go of that which does not serve you at the moment. Do not force yourself to accept anything that does not resonate with you at this time. Let yourself be drawn to that which is nourishing, life giving, and helpful for you. Let yourself gently let go of that which does not feel like it is a part of your path right now. This includes any teachings, understandings, images, and Light Beings that you may encounter on this path. You are sitting down to a great feast. Take time to choose what truly nourishes you.

We do suggest that, on your first time through the Great Passage, you experience each meditation in the order in which it was delivered to the world. These meditations came through in a very intentional way, each one building on the ones that came before. Allow yourself time with each meditation. Let it transmit its teachings to you. Let it guide you when the time is right to move on to the next one. While short teachings are offered before each meditation, you may be called to skip the teachings altogether and dive straight into the heart-journey that each meditation provides. Please feel free to do this! You can always come back to the teachings later, once you have experienced the meditations on your own first.

Once you have stepped on each stone in turn, and arrived safely to the other side, we invite you to revisit these meditations at any time and in any order. Fly, dance, jump and alight on any stone that you feel drawn to. These meditations are encoded like a spiral, and each time you return to them you will emerge with something new to guide you on your journey.

These meditations offer a deep and irreversible dive into your holy depths. Do not underestimate the power of the full-bodied transformation you are undertaking. We ask you, then, to listen closely to the guidance of your Higher Self. If at any time you feel destabilized or overwhelmed by the process, trust that it is time to set it aside for the moment, to integrate what has come to you. There is no need, in this New World, to force your way into knowing. It happens inevitably, for each of us on our own timeline. This journey will always be here, the path is laid in front of you. There is no need to rush or to walk it all at once. Let yourself rest and integrate as needed.

We hear the call of the prophecies

And turn our ears inward to listen,

Ready now for the story of our own

Divine Oneness to be revealed

Prophecies

This book is a manifestation of prophecies seeded long ago. As we read, we stand at the convergence of these prophecies. They come together now, a juncture of wide, flowing rivers carrying potent memories of our original birth. We drink the waters of these rivers and remember the ancient lands on which we stood. We remember a time of harmony and peace, of oneness and joy, when our hearts beat in time with the rhythm of the earth. We remember when we spoke the same language – a language of love and laughter and recognition. We anoint ourselves with the waters of these converging prophecies and feel the layers of illusion wash from our eyes. We see clearly the magic shining forth from every whirling leaf, every bird, and every passing face. Each humble stone under our feet tells a story of long ago, when all on earth lived as one being. We hear the call of these prophecies and turn our ears inward to listen, ready now for the story of our own divine oneness to be revealed.

Mary Magdalene appears on the wave of this convergence, standing at the apex of the confluence of prophecies. She is the tolling bell, calling us out of the illusion of our lives. She shines like a star in the darkness, beckoning us to leave behind the flimsy imprisonment of fear. She is a beacon, a tower of strength and light. She is the centrepoint of these prophecies, bringing them into being through the power of our collective faith. As we stand together, she anoints us in the waters of life that pour like a sparkling rainbow stream from her open hands. We feel the blessing of light that is our birthright. With Illumined Hearts we claim the inheritance of joy and abundance and love that has been passed to us, hand to hand, by our loving ancestors.

Like a Gardener of Light walking the earth, Mary Magdalene sowed the seeds of our resurrection during her incarnation. She brings us together now, all of us who walk the Way of Love, to harvest the yield of those shining seeds watered through the ages by our devotion. We come to eat of the bread of life and share it joyfully amongst ourselves. The abundance of the New Earth is upon us. The message of the New Earth is one of joy and peace, simplicity and naturalness. We speak it aloud as one voice that flows from the eternal wellspring of our hearts.

Mary Magdelene reminds us that the New Earth dwells within each of us. It cannot be accessed by the brash searchlight of our thinking mind, but must be beckoned forth from the shining invitation of hope, of peace, of joy, of generosity, of love within our united, sacred heart.

The time of the prophecy is now.
The New Earth has arrived.
It is time now to claim it.

Part 2

The Eight Meditations

Before you arcs a glittering Rainbow Bridge. It spans the waters of life, a shining river of starlight, sunlight, and cosmic light, shimmering in swirling eddies. As you look closer, you see that the bridge is made of eight crystal stepping stones, connected with shining rays of light.

Each stone is a different shape, colour, and size. Their borders are not solid, but shift and transmute before your eyes.

On the far bank of the river you see a Being enrobed in light. This Being shines with all of the colours of the earth. It moves with grace and ease, walking lightly upon the emerald ground. Behind the Being stretches a vast unknown terrain. You know that this far land is unmapped, untrodden, never before seen by human eyes.

That Being on the far bank is you. The land beyond is the adventure of your life, stretching into infinity. It lies just beyond the Great Passage of this Rainbow Bridge.

Eagerness and anticipation rise in your heart and thrum in your blood as you gaze upon this Being of Light, a shining star come to earth. You smile in anticipation of reunion with that Being: your True Divine Self. Your mind opens in wonder and joy to the promise of magic, adventure, and discovery of the land stretching just beyond the far bank.

The Opening Ceremony and First Meditation

Preparation for the Opening Ceremony

Welcome to the opening ceremony of the Great Passage. Welcome to this most sacred moment of intention, connection and peace. This ceremony brings you gently into the transformative field of this book. You are about to enter into a river, stepping into an energetic flow of miracles that will carry you into a new space of transformation. Before moving into the space of the opening ceremony, we offer you guidance here on what to anticipate and how to let yourself be fully held within the loving field of your own Great Passage.

Preparation of Space

Before you begin the ceremony, take the time to prepare yourself and your space. This is a time that is just for you. Allow yourself to create an environment around you that is sacred, quiet, and focused. Arrange yourself and your surroundings in whatever way feels most nurturing and loving to you. You may want to light a candle, create a nest of blankets and pillows, bless a glass of drinking water, make a sacred cup of tea, or set up a small altar that you arrange with meaningful objects. Take a few deep breaths and allow yourself to see, feel, and absorb the way in which you are caring for yourself in this moment. Immerse yourself in the tenderness of self-love and self-care that you are bringing to yourself. Perhaps you spend a lot of time caring for others. It is time to direct that energy inward now. It is time to connect to your Higher Self, the part of you that will help you gently navigate in the most perfect way, through this Passage to the New Earth.

The Sacred Space of the Heart

The ceremony will introduce you to the Sacred Space of your Heart. Your heart space is a quantum sanctuary of light, love, and infinite wisdom. This is the place where all good and pure things manifest in your life, and in which your whole history is written. Once you know the way, you can return again and again whenever you need to be held in the universal arms of love and grace. As you enter the Sacred Space of your Heart, you will, without needing to do anything, be given all that you need. Your divine heart is the part of you that is eternal, still, peaceful, and unchanging.

You are a being of love and light, and from the Temple of Your Heart you will feel the truth of this declaration. Though you may have some experiences already, the incredible heart power that is the basis of your divine architecture will reveal itself to you more and more, as you regularly inhabit the Sacred Space of your Heart. Your heart is like a unicorn – magic and mysterious. It is an all-powerful, vast, unmapped space of creation. But all that is to be discovered through the inner revelatory path as you move forward through this Sacred Passage.

From your enlightened heart you can connect to the hearts of every person who ever has, and ever will, move through the initiation of this Passage. As you connect to these luminous souls that shine like stars all over the globe, let it resonate that you have entered a community of light and love. In the company of these guardians and way-showers of infinite cosmic source intelligence, you will never again need to feel like you are working alone. By stepping into a community anchored in the One Heart Consciousness, you enter a portal of heart power unlike any other. When only two beings gather for sacred work, then the field of miracles opens. When thousands gather together, a creation force is activated that changes the very fabric of reality; new worlds are created effortlessly.

As you enter this ceremony, let yourself find your place within this family of humans and all other beings who live within the field of unconditional love. These are your brothers and sisters who are committed to bringing the Sophia Christ Consciousness to the planet. You will feel their presence when connecting to the Sophia

Christ grid that encircles the earth. As you touch and become part of the grid with your own light, you will see or feel it amplify in response to your intention.

This is a grid drawing energy from the Great Central Sun – the highest and purest consciousness.

Mother Earth and Father Sky

As you enter the ceremony, you will be welcomed into the open arms of your Divine Mother Earth and Father Sky. They have been waiting for so long to hold you. Find your place as the precious child of these two divine beings as, together, the three of you make the Holy Trinity. Through their Divine Love, they mirror your own Divine Love. Ultimately, you are them ... sacred duality bringing forth pure divine life. Through their perfection and grace they mirror the perfection and grace of your being.

The Seven Directions and the Five Elements

Bring yourself into resonance with the seven directions. As you read or listen, let their presence wash over your heart. Feel the loving presence of the East, which brings to you the fresh glow of new beginnings, infinite possibilities, friendship and illumination. Feel the loving presence of the South, which brings you the soft winds of compassion, and life's vital force. The South brings in the qualities of enlightenment, playfulness, and a sense of wonder and passion.

Let yourself be embraced by the presence of the West, which holds you in the deep knowing that you are enough. It reminds you that the infinite cycle of life consists of dissolution of old and a return of new manifested intention. Let yourself be embraced by the presence of the North, which carries with it the divine wisdom of the universal teachers, the field of universal spiritual wisdom from all dimensions, abundance and inspiration.

As you bring your attention to the earth below you, let yourself feel what it means to be fully met in all that you are, just as the earth rises to meet you with every step you take. And as you bring your attention upwards to the infinite sky, let yourself expand into the limitlessness of your own potential. In drawing your attention inwards to your heart, let the true softness of your being envelop you in a field of love.

And now, bring yourself in contact with the five elements from which the whole material world is created, and which, when balanced, bring harmony to your life experience. Evoke fire, the element of burning, of alchemy, of heat, purification, and transformation. Evoke air, the element of presence, spirit and breath. Evoke water, the cleansing element of life, the element that remembers all, and connects all life with the Source. Evoke earth, the element of solidity, stability, and grounding. And evoke ether, or prana, the ineffable element that sustains your spirit.

Our Guides

This ceremony calls in the presence of our overlighting guides for this Passage. We call in these guides because they hold the energy of the New Earth. They help us move our resonance into harmony with their own light and energy. Together we create a safe channel to be in, to work in, and to awaken through.

These guides each offer a different quality and frequency of Divine Love, and each guide plays a different role in our Passage into unity consciousness.

Feel this Passage as a symphony. As you immerse yourself you can let yourself hear the voice, tenor, soprano, and resonance of each over-lighting guide as they tone their voices and frequencies in each of the initiations, either in the forefront or in the background.

At the centre of the orchestra is Mary Magdalene. She is the maestra of this Passage, conducting the symphony with perfect grace, timing, unconditional love and patience. Feel her presence. She is the Rainbow Divine Feminine, holder of Sophia Christ Consciousness. She sees you and loves you unconditionally. She welcomes you into this Passage of Light. Mary Magdalene is the rising power of the sacred feminine – in union with her beloved Yeshua – and she holds the frequencies for your divine transformation into Oneness.

Feel and connect to Yeshua, her beloved. He is at her side, and they are One. He is her Twin Ray, her Divine Masculine mirror. He holds the field of this Passage with perfect cosmic light, love and grace. He walks at Mary Magdalene's side in harmony, devotion, with the impeccable execution of Divine Will. He stands by her side as she masterfully and divinely orchestrates this collective Passage into Higher Consciousness. While present, Yeshua acts in the background as a figure of support and devotion to the shining light of his Beloved.

Grandmother Anna, Mother Mary, and the Family Line of David are present throughout the Passage. They carry knowledge of ancient mystery school lineages, teachings, and codes of awakening.

Sophia, the Mother of all Creation, is present. She is the field from which this Passage emerged, and she is the Passage itself and everything in it.

Archangel Metatron is present with Lord Melchizedek & the Melchizedek Beings. Together they hold the wisdom of the MerKaBa and the Light Body, which were kept secret in the Darker Times of Humanity. They are here to empower us, to initiate us into our own spiritual mastery and lead us to collective unification.

The Arcturians and Pleiadians are with us. They are interdimensional healers from the higher dimensions of unconditional love, who can remove any negative energy that exists in the field. The Arcturians are masters of cosmic architecture and have been helping humanity since eons. They are capable of transmuting the densest energies existent on this earth, when they are asked to do so.

The Council of Whale Elders is present. They hold the records of Gaia in the Light Matrix from the beginning of time.

The Lemurian High Council, the Lemurians, and Light Beings from Inner Earth, Agartha, and Telos are present. They are our brothers and sisters of the fifth and higher dimensions, guiding us through the ascension process. With the Arcturians and Pleiadians, they also offer DNA healing and repair. Among others, they know how to restore our DNA strands to their original state, as they were in the first eras of earth.

The Great White Brotherhood – a group of perfected beings of great spiritual power – is present.

Traveller and the circle of 13 crystal skulls from Peru are present. They are Divine Intergalactic Light Beings who are helping humanity through the crystal skull technology.

The Galactic Federation of Light is present, bringing divine representatives from across our galaxy.

Archangel Michael and the great Angelic Realms are present, holding space in devotion, trust, and competence for the perfect completion of this Passage.

Babaji, the Divine Father in his incarnated form, is present to support this transformational Passage. Babaji, the Immortal, has lived on earth for many thousands of years in various physical embodiments.

We also feel the presence of the Earth Kingdoms: the Animal Kingdom, the Plant Kingdom, the Mineral Kingdom, and the Elementals. These realms have come in to support us and the ascension of Gaia into the field of Christ Consciousness, because we are all ascending together. In so doing, we are entering a New Era of Oneness marked by conscious cooperation between the realms, in which each realm shares its gifts for the benefit of the whole. We feel their love, we recognise their soft, gentle and powerful energy, and send our love back.

We now invite you to call in your own guides. Know that simply by speaking their names from your heart, they will come to your work and will remain present throughout your journey.

As you nestle into your space, feel the field of silence settle around you like a warm blanket. As you prepare for your Passage, let a pure and loving intention for this journey rise up from the centre of your being. Speak it aloud from the pure space of your heart. Allow yourself to feel the magic and anticipation of this divine moment. It is time now to relax and receive.

Teachings of the First Meditation

The opening ceremony moves seamlessly into the first meditation. As you allow yourself to be carried on the gentle tide of these words, you slip easily from the opening ceremony into the prepared space of your first guided journey.

This first meditation prepares you for all that is to come in this Passage, introducing you to the latent power within you to receive and illuminate the divinity of your own soul.

The meditation begins with a single ray of solar diamond light. It is unnamed, from an unknown source. This light enters your heart like the first finger of dawn reaching from the long-held darkness of a horizon that has, until now, been hidden from our sight. The ray rises to meet you, illuminating gently the landscape of your inner terrain. Allow this loving ray into your heart and behold, with reverence and awe, the dawning of your own illumined self.

As you receive the light of this ray, you naturally become the light, and your own body begins to glow with its own self-sustaining illumination. This meditation guides you to expand your light beyond what you have perceived as the fixed contours of the Self. You see how easily you can light up the entire earth simply with the power of your divine intention. With the will of the cosmos behind and within you, you see how effortlessly your own intentions become manifest as the Light of the Earth.

Once you have been introduced to the effortless power of your own Inner Light, Mary Magdalene comes to you. She comes to you in her own Light Body to act as a reflection, a mirror of your own. With her very being she shows you the latent power that shines within you – to live and walk as a sun on Gaia.

Take her proffered cup and let its golden liquid cleanse you. It flows into your being with a divine intelligence, seeking the places within you that thirst for illumination and love. This liquid purifies you, preparing your body for what is to come. Feel the way it loosens all that is tight and constricted, feel the way it vibrates within, the way it unclasps your thinking mind from that which it would hold onto, out of fear.

And then, once you have partaken of this alchemical offering, you are given space to simply observe, in silence, in reverence, the divine majesty of your own inner being. Perhaps you have never beheld it before. Perhaps you haven't in a long time honoured the deep and abiding divinity of your soul. Allow yourself to do this now in the deep and gentle arms of your inner silence.

Watch, then, as your in-dwelling divinity rises and spills over into all of your bodies from the inside out. As you turn your attention back to your physical body, remember that you have imbibed the Alchemical Golden Light of Divine Love, and you are now and always gold – precious, shining, and rare. Take time then to let this understanding sink into the very cells of your body.

Let yourself sink now into the welcoming arms of this meditation. Slip into the warm current of the words, and let yourself be carried into the loving embrace of all those who have gathered to celebrate this Great Passage.

The Opening Ceremony
&
First Meditation

*You are invited to get comfortable for this opening ceremony.
Find a place and a way to sit or lie down, whatever you prefer,
but find a place and a way to stay alert while taking this journey.*

*See if you can hold your spine straight, as straight as possible,
without forcing anything. And take a moment to bring all of your
attention inside of yourself, to observe your body. Just scan your
body and observe it in a neutral way. All is fine. All has its place.*

*And when thoughts come in, just observe them and let them pass,
like softly drifting clouds in the sky.*

Now slowly bring your attention to your breath. Observe your breath – in and out, at a rhythm that is natural for you. Don't force anything, just breathe in a very natural way, in a way that is good for you. If you feel you want to take a really deep breath and exhale strongly, please do so. With each exhale, breathe out all tension and stress, and any ideas about the past or the future. Just let them all go.

If there are still stresses or blockages inside of your body, this is the moment to release them. Release all energy-chords to the outside world and any stories from your daily life and routines. And as you do, feel how you become more and more centered in yourself. Allow yourself to fully arrive in this most sacred moment, in the Eternal Now.

Slowly bring your intention to the Space of your Heart. This is the place where the purest part of you resides. This is a place of deep silence, love, and light. Your purest intentions arise from here. Feel this space of love and radiance. And feel how much love you hold.

And from this space of love, bring your attention to Gaia, and connect with her. Gaia provides you with all you need and more. Send all your love to her! And you will immediately feel how she responds. She will always send you her infinite love. You are her beloved child. Feel the interaction between you and Mother Earth – your planet, your home at this time.

Now bring your attention back to the space of the heart, and then to Father Sky – the eternal sky, which is all around us, the big, big, blue sky. Send love from the space of your heart to Father Sky, your Heavenly Father. And feel how Father Sky responds immediately, sending his love back to you. You are his beloved child.

Feel the interaction with Father Sky, the infinite sky above you, and Gaia, Mother Earth. Feel how you are exactly in the middle of these two forces, the child of the two. And their love flows through you. You are the Divine Light that is created from these two.

Now bring your attention to the Sacred Space of your Heart. Connect to its purity, and to that part of you that has always been there and will always be there. Connect to that purest part of you.

And from this place of purity, reconnect to all of the people and all of the beings in this network of light. There are people from all around the globe, from all around Planet Earth. Everywhere across Gaia, human beings are making this Great Passage. So from heart to heart, we bring the light to each other and we create this infinite web of Love & Light.

Observe as the light amplifies, and as the field of love becomes bigger and bigger as this channel is prepared for the amplification of the Sophia Christ Consciousness. And as we stand across the planet, all united, consciously connect to the Christed grid that is around and in the earth. It's the most beautiful crystalline grid that holds the highest consciousness from the Central Galactic Sun and beyond. It is constructed from Source energy. You are invited to deeply connect with this grid. You are a part of this grid.

And while the grid amplifies and amplifies, connect to this one big circle, to this big network, and evoke the 7 directions.

Evoke the East, the South, the West, and the North. Evoke the downward direction, and the upward direction, and the direction within.

Evoke the 5 elements – the Fire, the Water, the Earth, the Air and the Ether.

Observe how the directions and the elements are part of our directionality on earth.

And in the centre of our circle of light, welcome and honour the presence of Mary Magdalene and her beloved Yeshua.

While they remain at the centre of our circle, call in Archangel Metatron, Archangel Michael and all of the Angelic Realms. Ask them to be with us, to guide us, and to protect us with a circle of light while you work in this channel and beyond.

Call in the Divine Mother, the Sophia of all Creation.

Call in the Pleiadians, the Arcturians, the Council of the Whale Elders, the Lemurian High Council, the Lemurians and Light Beings from Inner Earth, the Brotherhood of Light, Traveller and the Circle of Crystal Skulls, the Galactic Federation of Light, and Babaji.

They are all here to support this process, the process of you coming into Christed Consciousness.

Now call into our circle all those who you would like to invite to support this process. Call in those helpers that you are used to working with, the ones you have a special relationship to...

As you feel your place in this grid of light and your connection to all the others, reach out also to the Animal Kingdom, the Plant Kingdom, the Elemental Kingdom, the Mineral Kingdom, and to all life on earth in the visible and less visible realms. Send your Love & Light to all of them.

And in the centre of this circle arises a ray of the most brilliant, multifaceted, solar, diamond light. This is a vertical ray that comes all the way from the Central Galactic Sun and connects to the centre of Gaia. It moves through the centre of this circle, where Mary Magdalene and Yeshua are standing. They hold this ray.

Observe this most brilliant ray, which holds so much cosmic intelligence. Connect your heart space to this ray of light and feel how the purest of light enters your Light Body. This cosmic intelligence is here to help you in your awakening process.

You are invited to receive this light. Open up and allow it to enter your bodies. Allow the process to be guided by Mary Magdalene and Yeshua, so that it moves as it should move, at a pace that is optimal for you. You receive exactly what you are here to receive at this time.

And while your heart is being filled with this purest light, you see that this light from the heart space expands into all your bodies.

And you feel as it purifies your system. If you feel any more blockages, you guide the light into these knots, to allow them to transmute. This light is an alchemical light that has the intelligence of re-aligning everything back with the Divine. So guide the light to a place where you feel it is still needed, with the intention of purification, healing, and full alignment with your divine coding, your purest DNA.

And now amplify this light outside of your body, in the place where you are. And feel that you become a radiant sun, a light being radiating light and love into your environment. Start with the place where you are right now and slowly increase the radiation of your inner solar light, so it radiates more and more amply into the village, town or city you are in, and into the nature around you.

Make it even bigger so that it radiates all across your country and your continent. And let it radiate everywhere – into the waters and the air ... Let it shine everywhere! Let it shine in all directions! As you make it bigger and bigger, you shine your solar light across all of Gaia.

And you see and feel how the Angelic Realms support you, and how they amplify the light. You sense how they protect you as Gaia becomes ONE solar light planet in the galaxy. And while you observe your solar-powered planet, you feel that your inner solar force and the outer solar force are all one and the same. You hold this radiance inside of your heart, in your consciousness, and you shine this purest light everywhere. You are a Beacon of Light! And you carry the codings for this time, to make the change happen on Gaia.

From here, come back to the Space of your Heart and connect with the light ray at the centre of our circle. This is the moment that Mary Magdalene, in her Light Body, comes towards you to bring you the cup of purification. When she is with you, you are invited to take this cup with the golden liquid of purification and to drink it with the intention that this purification is for your highest good. In so doing, you receive The Blessing – The Fulfilment of the Promise.

In deep gratitude, you return the cup and you observe your heart space. You observe your inner being. You feel the connection to all of the people in this Passage, and the connection to all who have the same intention of the highest good for Gaia and the Galaxy. Connect with them, feel the strength of being together, and be aware that you hold this channel in this Christ grid consciously. You can return here any time you want.

For now, you are invited to pay your respects to all the beings in this network, to thank Mary Magdalene and Yeshua for their guidance, and to honour all of the Light Beings that are around you, and who will continue, loyally and lovingly, to support you. Show them deep gratitude for being a part of this process, and for showing up in full presence. Come back to the Space of your Heart, where your intense light resides. And connect to the silence of this place. There is a deep, deep silence, which is at the source of your existence.

Slowly come back to the consciousness of your body. Bring your attention to your physical body and feel or scan your body. Slowly start moving your fingers and your toes, really gently. This body of gold, your divine vehicle in life – is your most precious gift from Gaia. So be really gentle with it as you start moving, and feel how the golden light energy is still in each and every particle in your body. The tiniest bits of yourself are made of divine energy. Move very slowly. Start moving your arms and your legs. You may want to touch or massage some parts of your body.

And whenever you are ready, but take your time, slowly open your eyes. Bring your attention back to the space where you are sitting. Look around the space where you are, and at the same time, keep your attention focused in the inner realms, simply being aware of the outer realms. Keep your sense of this golden light inside of you, as you are looking out. Slowly, come fully back into the physical realm.

Please take your time. Gently breathe in and out, until you are fully back, feeling the strength returning to your body and knowing that you are ready to move into your daily life again. Take your time; don't rush. If you feel you want to do this meditation again, during the day or the week, please do so. Keep observing from a neutral place what is happening inside of you.

We wish you the most wonderful day!

Thank you for being with us!

Namaste.

The Second Meditation: Forgiveness of the Divine Mother

Teachings of the Second Meditation

This meditation beckons you into the peaceful arms of the Divine Mother. Feel the golden softness of her love as it surrounds you. In her embrace, all is well. Her love is soft velvet, cradling you like a precious jewel. In this place of warmth and tenderness, you feel safe to let go of all that you have been carrying. Sink into the simplicity and ease of this meditation as it guides you into the effortless practice of releasing that which doesn't serve your highest self. The Mother holds out her arms in an invitation to forgive. You no longer have to wait to forgive or to be forgiven. Forgiveness can happen now, immediately, in the moment. When you feel the hands of the Divine Mother gently freeing you from all that is heavy, you can allow yourself to sink into the simple rapture of your own lightness of being.

Releasing

This meditation shows you how easy it can be to release painful lower frequencies into the Divine Mother's field of unconditional love. First you become conscious of the frequencies – these feelings or thoughts that tug you downwards into a place that feels too small and heavy for you. As you allow the Divine Mother to show you her Way of Love, you become more and more sensitive to the subtlest disturbances in thought or emotion.

When we enter the field of the Divine Mother, all that is painful will naturally lift to the surface to be cleared into her waiting arms – arms of patience, understanding, compassion and transmutation. The Divine Mother is an infinite field of compassion and can transmute any aspect of pain into love, while holding space for you. All that you are ready to release will come forward to be cleared. You may feel an echo of the pain, but you can relax, knowing that you are safe and held, and that whatever is troubling you has a place to go.

The Divine Mother lives, at all times, within you as the voice of your heart. Many of us have lost touch with this heart-voice, this sacred inner navigation system. As we've grown up, we have absorbed other voices. These voices deny our divinity. The voice of the Divine Mother within you is never critical, judgmental, harsh, angry, or defeated. She offers only loving words and empowering, uplifting truths. She always sees who you truly are: a divine and precious being, a perfect expression of your soul.

You will return again and again to her frequency. Soon you will be able to feel it through the noise of the world. As the field of your own compassion grows, it becomes easier and easier to recognize and release all that does not reinforce self-love.

Immerse yourself in this gentle field of infinite compassion and light. Begin now to tune into her frequency of limitless love and care. As you read or listen to the meditation, feel the softness of her love. She loves you, her precious child. She knows your name and everything about you. She knows your dreams and your deepest longings. She sees the way you carry your burdens and your pain. She knows the ways you have turned away from love. She sees all of it. She joyfully and tenderly brings you back, over and over again, to the essence of your deepest being – the love and peace that have woven your soul into a glowing masterpiece of light.

The Truth of Self

The Divine Mother will show you the meaning of both compassion and unconditional love. Feel as these qualities come together in your body, as they connect deeply with each other, opening you like a flower opens with the warmth of the sun's rays.

Feel her compassion, as she meets you in every state of being and points you again and again to your highest expression of Self. Compassion is the harvest of wisdom – that deep, experiential knowing of human suffering.

Feel her unconditional love as an ocean of softness that carries you effortlessly into your highest state of being. Unconditional love is the resonance of the heart. It is the field of life from which all things arise. In the field of unconditional love, all is one. All is perfect.

As a human, you are gifted with the power to hold both compassion and unconditional love within you. This is a gift that humanity offers to the universe. You have traversed times of darkness, yielding rare and precious wisdom that shines like a jewel through time and space. Your heart rests in the light of unconditional love. In cupped hands, you offer this wisdom and unconditional love, through the pure universal waters, to all beings thirsty for truth, light, and love.

The Mother sees your True Self. You are a holy child of light. This is your True Self, the self that has always existed and always will. You are a Living Grail, a ray of hope and joy.

Sometimes you will not feel that you are this holy child. These are the times when Mother waits to remind you of who you truly are. The field of the Mother is both the place where you can rest and the place where you can grow. It is your foundation and your sanctuary. It is where you can return to again and again when the world presses in on you. She wants nothing more than to bring you into the sanctuary of her loving arms. This sanctuary exists in your own perfect Sacred Heart, and it is always open to you. When you have lost your way, ask her to lead you here. When you feel abandoned, hurt, or in doubt, call on the Divine Mother and she will hold you in perfect peace.

Forgiveness

From within this sanctuary, you will be guided to forgive. When you allow yourself to forgive, you let yourself be cleansed of your burdens. You liberate yourself from carrying another's story, and you put yourself at the centre of your sacred soul contract and hero's journey. You disentangle an inter-wovenness of stories that are not serving your highest path. You allow others to follow their own stories, while you move into the highest version of your own. Your body, and theirs, are liberated so that fresh energy and impetus has room to emerge, aligned with the highest, divine awareness.

The Mother has been waiting to welcome you into her field so she can take your weary load from you. You may feel pain arise in you as you prepare to let go. Know that her field is a safe, gentle place for you to feel all you need to feel in order to let it go. There is no judgment of you and no criticism, only infinite love and care. As you release your burdens into the field of unconditional love, it will leave a space of emptiness within you. That space is a holy vessel prepared to be filled with the Divine Mother's light and love. Let her fill you, nourish you, and heal all of the places that have become empty of pain.

We remind you, too, of the family of light that surrounds you as you prepare to enter her loving embrace. You are not alone and never will be again. May we all rise together as one group of love in this beautiful field that is open for us in this channel of love, light and forgiveness.

Feel the Light Beings holding their arms to you and radiating love from hearts as bright as sunlight. You can call on them at any time for support or guidance. See in your inner eye the pure light of your heart, and of the hearts of your vast family of light. Allow that image to rest on your inner eye for a moment as you move into your meditation.

The Second Meditation

You are invited to close your eyes now, to take a few deep breaths, and to draw your energy from the outer world to the inner world, to your inner temple. With each inbreath and outbreath, become more and more internal, focussing all your energy into the inner realms.

Breathe in, and breathe out, slowly sinking into ever-greater stillness.

And when you feel that all of your energy has come back to you, and that you are holding it in the inner planes, then slowly become conscious of Gaia, Mother Gaia. Send her your love and gratitude for being able to be here, to be here in this earth home, with all the beautiful experiences you are able to have here, in this paradise. Send her your love and gratitude and she will send you her love back, because you are her child. She will do anything for you. And as you feel this love come into your heart, just feel that beautiful relationship, that sacred relationship.

And then become conscious of the love that you have for your Heavenly Father, your Cosmic Father, and your eternal journey throughout creation. Feel gratitude for your eternal life, in this realm and others. You will soon receive love back from your Heavenly Father, as you are his child.

You are the child of these two beings, and together, you form the Holy Trinity. Feel as their energy nurtures you, and feel their love towards you and your love towards them.

Now you are going to make a voyage into the Sacred Space of the Heart. If you do not know how to go directly to the Sacred Space of the Heart, or have not had the experience yet, imagine yourself standing behind your physical heart. Your heart is in front of you; you are behind your heart. And there, a vortex will be revealed to you. Just very simply step into that vortex, which is a wormhole into the Sacred Space of your Heart. Allow yourself to be pulled effortlessly into this most sacred place.

Again, start from behind the heart, allow the vortex to reveal itself, step into the vortex, and allow yourself to be pulled into the Sacred Space of the Heart. If it is dark when you arrive there, then just ask that the light be put on. See, sense or feel how it is to be in this space. Feel the quality of peace, of stillness, in this sacred space, in this inner temple. Take some time to explore this peaceful space. This is a space where all is well.

Mother Mary, Mary Magdalene, Kwan Yin, or any other emanation of the Divine Mother, in her pure essence, is here to take care of you in this most sacred space, today. She is here to care for you, to nurture you, to hold you, to replenish you with Divine Love. She loves you more than you could ever imagine. Feel this most beautiful healing energy that she bathes you in. And when you have expanded this golden healing energy through your heart, then allow it to go to your whole physical body, to move through your emotional body, your mental body, as well as to heal your soul.

We carry many traumas at the level of the soul from a broken heart in this and past lifetimes, and this broken heart, this soul trauma, can now be healed. Feel this most beautiful, sacred field. It is time to give over to the Divine Mother, all your suffering caused by thousands of years of patriarchal abuse. All men and all women have suffered under systemic abuse of the patriarchy, of the corrupted patriarchy, and the Divine Mother asks you to give her all this suffering now, so that you can be set free.

The pain is very deep. Allow this sacred golden energy to take it all away. You may still be experiencing this pain in an intimate relationship, a family relationship, a work relationship, or through the broader corrupt political and social systems. At this time, allow yourself to forgive those who have trespassed against you, and by doing so, you set yourself free. Allow all the pain to be washed away, so that you can take back your energy to use it creatively in a way that supports your evolution now.

Stay in this healing field. You don't need to know the story. No analysis is needed. Just open as much as possible to receiving this healing energy. We will stay in silence for a few moments to bathe in this sacred energy.

If, at any moment, it feels impossible to forgive, ask Mother Divine to help you. This is about YOU liberating yourself, taking back your energy, to direct it in a way that serves YOUR evolution right now.

There is nothing that the Divine Mother cannot do. Just allow her to cleanse you. Allow her to set you free!

Once this energy has worked fully through your system, feel the divine bliss in your heart, then in all the cells of your body. Allow this bliss to radiate outwardly to your family, to your neighbours, to your co-workers, and then further across the planet. Allow it to bathe all of Gaia. This energy is pure ecstatic bliss and freedom.

You are a sovereign soul, preparing yourself to embody at deeper and deeper levels the Sophia Christ consciousness. Allow yourself to feel this field of unconditional love that is the very essence of who you are.

Now direct this essence to nourish the Christ grid all around Gaia. Amplify this unconditional golden love and light to illuminate this grid, to amplify this energy on Gaia.

When you feel this energy has been amplified as much as possible, creating the Golden Earth, slowly start to draw your attention back to yourself, to the Sacred Space of your Heart. How is it there now?

When you are ready to come back fully, start to gently wiggle your fingers and your toes, and draw a few deep breaths. Stretch a little bit, slowly, consciously, bringing your focus back to your body. And when you are ready to come back to the material world, gently open your new eyes.

Walk in the sacredness

of this field of Divine Love & Light,

and may your day be blessed.

The Third Meditation:
Journey to the
Temple of Illumination

Teachings of the Third Meditation

A World of Light

Welcome to the Third Meditation.

Prepare your heart with joy to enter a vast world of miracles and infinite possibility. This world is not imaginary. You are deeply connected to this world, as is every other being in the universe. Through this meditation, you will be gently introduced to new dimensions of Self. The important thing is to relax and allow all that comes. Let yourself be guided, and trust that so much is happening for you even if you are not, at present, consciously aware of it.

This meditation was brought through a field of immense joy, and the guides overseeing your journey through this meditation are so excited to be working with you.

As you move through this voyage, the feeling is one of inexpressible joy, pride, and excitement. It is likely that you will encounter that which is new for you. Trust that your deepest Self knows how to move in and through the world you are about to enter. Though some of it may seem like strange new terrain, know that you are deeply protected. There is nowhere to fall but into the loving arms of your attentive guides. So, we invite you to enjoy the field of joy that is encoded in the journey of this meditation.

This one will bring you into the light realms of your inner planes. Once you enter the Sacred Space of your Heart, you will be taken to the shores of Lake Titicaca and introduced to the Divine Temple of Illumination. Here is where the Divine Feminine Council gathers to oversee the healing and needs of our planet.

This temple is not an imaginary place. It is real and can be accessed through your Light Body. The healing, wisdom, and guidance you will receive at this temple are real and will have profound effects on all of your bodies. Trust that you will see changes occurring in your everyday reality.

The meditation will show you how to enter the portal of your Sacred Heart. From this most sacred space, you can travel anywhere in the universe. You are truly unlimited! This is the first of many journeys we will take together on this path of ascension. For many of you it may be the first time you travel in your Light Body. It may be difficult to understand that, even though your physical body is staying in one place, there is a very real, tangible part of you that is traveling somewhere else on earth. You do not need to fully understand what is happening for the meditation to "work." Simply allow yourself to relax and surrender to the images and sensations that arise as you are guided, allow yourself to enter into your natural, expansive state of being.

Coming into Wholeness

Before you travel to the temple, you will be guided to call back the fragments of your soul that splintered away when you encountered trauma in this and other lifetimes. These "splinters" or "soul fragments" are the parts of you that have been forgotten through the ages, buried like treasures in the sands of time. At times, parts of you may have needed to be hidden in order to preserve the purity of their wisdom and light. Other parts may have been severed or shattered through traumatic experiences. You are now ready to remember (literally re-member) these aspects of Self and reclaim the full power of your divinity and light.

As you call back your soul fragments you will feel the unlimited power of your free will. You will see how the sacred tools of intention and declaration are used to heal your soul. Your voice is an instrument of creation, and when you use it in accordance with divine will, its powers of restoration are infinite. When you reclaim the forgotten aspects of Self, your soul will come into alignment with your higher purpose.

You can expect this meditation to continue working with you long after your immersion in it. You have truly set a remarkable process in motion! As your soul comes more and more into alignment, you may begin to notice changes in your daily life. Even if you're not fully aware of your soul's higher purpose yet, you will start to instinctively sense which choices are aligned and which are not. You will find yourself naturally releasing things that don't serve your higher purpose until, over time, your higher purpose becomes fully revealed to you.

Reclaiming the Self is a process of allowance and faith, a step-by-step (and sometimes leap-by-leap!) moving forward. Allow your Higher Self to determine the rhythm of your process and trust that all comes in perfect timing.

The Prophecy of Connection

All of the meditations in this Passage open you into deep connection with your soul family. This meditation will begin by guiding you to connect your heart to the hearts of all others in the Great Passage. These are brothers and sisters all over the globe who, like you, are committed to bringing in the New Earth.

For many of us, being deeply connected to so many others can be a new feeling. The old ways, which are passing away, created feelings of separation and aloneness. In contrast, the New Earth is a place of joyful communion with all other beings. Your journey through the Great Passage will invite you out of solitude and into community with all others on this path.

Experiencing true unity with others may feel unfamiliar and possibly uncomfortable at first. You can trust that this Passage, and your personal voyage, are held safely by many competent and devoted guides. As you connect with your brothers and sisters of light, you will learn that it is safe to love and to be loved. You will begin to trust in the joy and peace of being One with the others on the path. Over time, sharing your Divine Love will feel as natural as breathing. We will see that as we merge our light with the light of the earth and with all other beings, our own light is amplified beyond measure. Our purpose becomes unified. When we join together we become strong enough to lift the planet and all her life forms into the light. We enter a New World reality of transparency and equality among all living beings, and an intimacy that results from a life lived in peace and harmony.

Twin Ray Energy

As you enter the Temple of Illumination, you will learn that the Divine Feminine Council is supported in its work by its Twin Ray "partners". As the Twin Ray energy was very strong in bringing forward this meditation, you may pick up on its frequency. We will share a brief teaching here to provide context for you.

In short, the Twin Ray, (which can be perceived as a specific, encoded light ray that interacts with your Rainbow Light Body) is not only about coming together as the divine masculine and the divine feminine. The ultimate intention of the Twin Ray teaching is to create a path for transcending duality entirely. Beyond duality, we will see, is both unification and wholeness; we find Oneness Consciousness.

The Twin Ray, then, is a transpersonal ray. It contains qualities of the Christ Consciousness and is fully accessible to us as we open to receive increasing levels of divine light.

There has been much misconception about the idea of a Twin Ray partner, a Twin Flame. When we are able to open up to our Rainbow Body through a field of unconditional love, that's when our Twin Ray can appear. This may or may not be a physical encounter. The more important understanding is about receiving the energy, light, and intelligence that comes with the teachings of the encoded Twin Ray. So, in contemplating the Twin Ray, we invite you to go beyond the stories you may have heard about it. We invite you, instead, to enter the realms of universal intelligence that are accessible for all of us.

Pleiadian Healers

While not "on stage" in this initiation, we want to note that the Pleiadian healers were very strong guides in the creation of this journey and the field from which it emerged.

Several of the Native American indigenous nations are deeply connected to the Pleiadians, as many are descended from the Pleiadian star nations. The Pleiadians hold a deep love for and commitment to humanity and have been helping us evolve over the eons.

They are loving, joyful, and competent healers. We mention them so that you can open to receive the healing that they want to gift you with, in this meditation. A new photonic light is encoded in this journey, and the Pleiadians can be called on at any time to make your integration process easeful, joyful, and loving.

The Golden Rose

Finally, on your journey you will be given the gift of a Golden Rose. This is the first of many divine gifts that will be joyfully bestowed on you in this Passage. You may feel overwhelmed by the amount of love and generosity of the Light Beings you encounter. Trust that you are worthy and ready to receive all they have to offer. It is their greatest joy to give all they can to you to help you fulfil your heroic soul's purpose in this lifetime. Accepting these gifts is a declaration of your own worthiness to receive. Allow them to come to you with an open and receptive heart.

We wish to remind you that these are living meditations with encodings that support each and every one of you in the perfect balanced way. As you enter into the space of this meditation, it will bring all that you require or need in the moment. All that is asked of you is to allow and receive the healing that wants to come. You are perfectly safe, held, and cared for.

Preparing Yourself

This meditation will gently teach you a new way of experiencing the world. Its messages will spread through your being like a subtle perfume expanding through a garden. As always, let your joy and intuition guide you. If there are moments where you feel you cannot follow, or something else is happening inside of you, simply hold space or honour your individual process and stay nestled snugly in the sacred space of your beautiful heart.

So, we invite you to get yourself ready. Prepare yourself. Prepare your space. Make yourself comfortable wherever you are on this beautiful earth.

Take a moment to arrive in the space of silence, by breathing in, and breathing out.

The Third Meditation

Make yourself comfortable, wherever you are on earth,
and take a moment to arrive in the space of silence.

Breathe in and breathe out, in the most natural way, and feel the ease of this most natural movement inside of you. Take in the oxygen, take in the beautiful prana that nourishes your body. And in the prana of the breath, there is a deep silence that holds everything. Feel with every breath you are taking in, that you become more and more silent. You feel yourself anchor more and more into your True Self.

Connect with the space of silence inside of yourself. In this deep state of being, there is a great sense of spaciousness. When you feel that spaciousness, start to connect to all beings of light around the globe. As you take your unique position in this network of light, connect with all the others, heart to heart, in this field of love. Connect to all those moving through the Passage in these times of transition and to those who will be moving through it later.

You are moving through the Passage because you are now called. You are called to be here in this moment in time, in this Eternal Now. Connect your heart to the grid of love of all human beings around the globe. And feel how this grid is lighting up even stronger.

Around the globe, around this grid, and around this circle, there is a beautiful network of Light Beings and Angelic Beings that protect you, so that the prophecy can be fulfilled. The whole earth realm is being prepared for this Passage. The Archangels are present and many of the Angelic Realms are around you – the Pleiadeans, the Hathors, the Arcturians and many more.

And throughout this light grid, you are accompanied by
Ascended Masters who are here to guide this evolutionary
process. They are here to support you; they are so loyal to
humanity and to you! This is one big communion! This is the
community of the Brother- and Sisterhood of the New Earth!

And now Mary Magdalene and Yeshua welcome you. They are
deeply grateful that you are here and ready to take the journey.

Take a moment to feel the deep silence, the spaciousness and
the connection with your deepest source, Creator Sophia. And
from this place, bring your attention to the Sacred Space of your
Heart.

You are now invited to move into the space of your heart. If
you are used to going into the Sacred Space of the Heart, please
go in, in the way you prefer. If you are new to the Sacred Space
of the Heart, you are invited, as a first step, to bring your
awareness to the back of your physical heart. Do this easily, just
through intention. You will see your physical heart in front of
you. And when you are there, you will notice there is a vortex
into the heart. And this vortex will bring you inside the Sacred
Space of the Heart.

So, when you are ready, move closer to the vortex. You don't
have to do anything special. Just step into the vortex and you
will move through it effortlessly, into the Sacred Space of the
Heart. If this sacred space is dark when you arrive, then just ask
that the light be turned on. Observe what it is like to be in this
most sacred space, in this space of pure love.

You can move around it and observe what it is like here. It may
be empty, or you may notice people, pictures, objects or other
things in this space. Anything is possible in the Sacred Space of
the Heart. Just observe, no need to do anything else. You can
wander around a little bit if you wish, preparing yourself for the
next phase of the journey.

And now that you have fully arrived in the Sacred Space of the Heart, you are invited to move through this space to a most beautiful place in Nature, a place you feel is paradise. Take a look around, and witness the beauty of this place, on Gaia. It is a unique paradise in the Galaxy! And when you are ready, start to move deeper and deeper into this paradise. Notice that you are accompanied by your guides while you move.

You are now invited by Mary Magdalene to follow her in the direction of Peru. You may never have been to Peru before, but this does not matter. Just move inside your heart towards the place we now call Peru, and you are guided, with all the other human beings in this Passage, to the shores of Lake Titicaca. You are expected! This move from one place to another on earth through the inner realms is effortless. Just allow yourself, with intention, in a split second, to be there.

Many Light Beings and Ascended Masters have waited there for you, for eons. They are so delighted to see you and they warmly welcome you to the shores of this sacred lake.

As you move through a crowd of beings, who are welcoming you, you move towards the water. It is such a joy to be here! You, and so many others, have been waiting to come here for many lifetimes! You take a look out at this huge lake in front of you, with its deep blue waters. You remember that in this lake, Lake Titicaca, reside the Paradise Codes. The New Earth blueprint is encoded here.

You are guided to step onto a boat that is waiting for you to bring you to an island, a very special island. You step onto the boat and the boat moves slowly and gently over the waters, in the direction of a temple island. This is a very special etheric temple island.

And while you move over the water, you connect to the waters of Lake Titicaca. Maybe you want to touch the water, bless the water, drink the water, or do whatever you feel called to do, while you're travelling across the lake. This is the most sacred and precious water in this region on earth and it holds and shares a very deep memory and intelligence.

You now see the island rising in front of you. In this sacred place, you will shortly be welcomed into the most beautiful temple.

When the boat approaches the island, take a moment to observe the way the temple rises in front of your eyes. And when you step out of the boat, onto this sacred land, you see yourself, along with all the others in this Great Passage, making a big circle in front of the temple. There is a deep heart connection among all those in the circle. You feel how this space, on this island, is protected by the divine masculine energies.

In this sacred circle, you may sit or lie down. You are being prepared to enter the temple, the Temple of Illumination. In this temple, you will receive exactly the illumination that you are ready to receive at this time. Here, you will find Lady Nada, Mary Magdalene, Kwan Yin, Mother Mary, Grandmother Anna, Pallas Athena, Lady Portia, Lady Venus, Sophia and all of the board of the Divine Feminine Council. This is the place where they co-create together. And this is the place of harmonization, the harmonization of feminine and masculine energies. They all reside here, together with their Twin Ray partners.

They are ready to work with you – but before they do so, prepare to call back your power, the power you were granted in your earliest incarnations on earth. You are requested to fully call back the power of your soul. So while you are sitting or lying on the ground of this sacred island of illumination, you are invited to go inside of yourself, deep inside of your soul.

And you hear the following words:

I NOW call back all of my lost soul-fragments, my power and my light. (3x)

I NOW call back any vows, soul contracts or programs of the past or present, from this life or others, that are not for the highest good of all, and I relinquish them NOW. (3x)

I NOW call back any power or light that I have unwillingly given away, or that has been taken from me. (3x)

I NOW release any chords or attachments from this life or other lives. (3x)

I affirm this for the highest good of all. (3x)

And so it is... And so it is... And so it is.

Now feel your inner power growing, increasing. Feel your soul's journey. And be aware that you are guided and protected.

And while you are sitting or lying down, you connect deeply with the soul of Gaia by moving your attention to her inner core. Deep under the lake, under the island on Lake Titicaca, you connect to the diamond centre in the heart of Gaia. And there is a brilliance, a diamond brilliance in the centre of Gaia that you can pull up by breathing it in. Start breathing in the diamond light from the centre of Gaia and fill your body with this most incredible, nourishing light energy.

With every breath you take, Gaia offers you this beautiful crystalline light. All of the little particles have pearlescent colours, as they come up from the inside of the earth. And you breathe them in, to nourish your body. Let these particles fill you and fulfil you. With every breath, you feel your strength growing.

While you continue to breathe in unison with Gaia, connect now with the Great Central Sun, the sun behind our sun and many other suns. The Solar Central Sun. Connect with it through our sun, and breathe in its frequencies through your crown chakra. With every breath you take through your crown chakra, the purest of light enters your whole body. So, with every breath you take, through our own sun and through our galactic sun, take in the light that comes from the Great Central Sun. Breathe it into your system through your crown chakra. Let it find its way into your body, into the deepest particles of your being, into your cells, all the way down to your DNA, atoms and molecules.

This whole time, you are still deeply connected to Gaia. Keep breathing in the light from the Great Central Sun and feel how your solar plexus is becoming stronger and more and more enlightened. You might want to put your hands on your solar plexus to feel how you are increasing your inner power to be of service. You can stay in this position as long as you like.

And when you are ready to enter the temple, rise up and slowly move in its direction. Keep breathing and feel the intense light from the temple entering your body. Do as you are called to do. It is all fine.

When you enter the temple, you are welcomed by Lady Nada and you are guided to a place that is fully equipped for you. So follow where you are guided to go inside the temple. Here is where you will find one of the divine feminine beings to accompany you. It can be that you are given nourishment by the Divine Mother. It can be that you receive the intelligence of the Divine Mother. You may need and receive physical support from the Divine Mother. Or you may receive another kind of support.

Just follow your intuition, as you are guided to the chamber of your choice. Know that you are guided and observe what awaits you. Take a little moment to be in silence.

Feel wherever you are, how the energy of the Divine Mother, the energy of pure love and nourishment, is merging with your energy. It is the most beautiful, caring, soft energy that you can merge with.

It is now time for everyone to come together in the central space of the temple, which is held by the Great Mother. If you are still in one of the chambers, slowly leave that chamber, in order to move into the central space in the Temple of Illumination.

You arrive in a big hall, a big space that is radiating with violet and golden colours. It is the Hall of the Violet Ray, held by Lady Nada, Kwan Yin, Mary Magdalene, and Mother Mary. All the divine feminine beings that you know, on and around our earth, are assembled here. They are all here for you.

You join the others in a big circle and from the centre of the circle one of the beings that represents the Great Mother comes forward with a rose, a golden rose, especially for you. Accept it as a gift of grace for you and for your journey. These divine beings know who you are and they know your journey. It is now time to receive the rose and to fully stand in your most divine essence.

Pay your respect and gratitude to this group of divine feminine beings, and take the rose into your heart. Then slowly move out of the temple, toward the boat on Lake Titicaca. And when you are ready, board the boat, take one more look at this divine Temple of Illumination, and the boat slowly sets sail, away from the island.

It moves back across Lake Titicaca, and you feel the energy of the waters, and how it has changed. You look at the colour of the lake and feel its radiance. The waters may open up some memories. You may just feel a field of eternal bliss, joy at being here, all together with your soul family. And when you arrive on the shore, step back onto the land.

Now make yourself ready. Prepare yourself to leave this space, to bring your consciousness back to your body, your physical body. Keep your eyes closed and observe yourself from the inside. You might feel some small sensations of energy, or something else. Just observe, and breathe in and out, in your own rhythm, at your own pace.

And now breathe in and out deeper, three times. And when you exhale, really exhale from the deepest place in your body. Inhale and exhale deeply. Slowly start moving your body, moving your hands and your feet.

Start to move your head very slowly, and when you are ready, open your eyes and come back to the place you are sitting or lying down. Look around you and bring your attention to your physical body. Arrive back fully into your physical body. Observe all parts of your physical body. Feel it, touch it, and honour it.

And while doing so, become more and more aware of this beautiful physical vehicle that has been given to you, to journey on the earth plane. Stay where you are until you are fully back in your body and ready to move again. Stay as long as you wish, to integrate all the energies from this meditation.

You can do this meditation as often as you like.

We wish you a beautiful journey.

We thank you for being with us.

Namaste

The Fourth Meditation:
The Temple
of Divine Will and Love

Teachings of the Fourth Meditation

Welcome to the fourth meditation, the next crystal stone sewn into the rainbow bridge of your Passage.

This meditation, which emerged from a field of strength and power, is one of purification and release. It is important, as we make space for our new Self to emerge, that we allow ourselves to be cleared of all things that no longer serve. These "things" may take the form of implants, energies, and/or contracts. These "things" are not bad. Each of them has served a purpose in some way, but they are now ready to be released.

All creations perpetuate the consciousness from which they were created. As humans, we command the power of our sovereignty and our free will to create anything at all. There exist in our field and in the field of Gaia many frequencies and entities that were created from the consciousness of separation. These entities and frequencies, therefore, cannot help but perpetuate separation. These fear-based things are not anything to be afraid of. They cannot alter the truth of who we are – our perfect innocence and divinity is always and forever preserved. These entities and frequencies do, however, have the power to obscure our true nature and as we take notice of them, it is important to stay deeply anchored in the space of the heart. As we call on the powerful Christed beings to clear them from our field, we will uncover more and more of our deepest nature, which is, and always has been,

Love. It is important to remember that these fear- and separation-based energies are not "part" of us. As we release them in this initiation, we are not losing any part of ourselves.

Clearing them is a simple and straightforward process. Fear- and separation-based energies cannot survive the light of awareness, and they must submit to your free will. This is a universal law. Once you declare your intention to be free of them, they will be removed easily and cleanly. This will set into motion another deep process in your life, of healing and purification, as your will is carried out in all dimensions of your being.

It is a courageous act to confront the energies within you that are not of a Christed nature. It is not your "fault" that they exist in your field. They are nothing to be ashamed of. Some of the energies are simply the detritus of a long and adventurous soul journey. Many of these energies or contracts have appeared to serve you well in the past, but they no longer fit your purpose.

Some of these energies were ones that you took on before this lifetime. Some you may have simply picked up from the collective field that you are currently living in. In many ways, it doesn't matter where they came from or what they are. As you clear your own field, you will naturally move like a cleansing, purifying presence through all of Gaia. Your own inviolable purity will naturally restore order and balance wherever you go.

Each person called to the work of the Great Passage holds a key that is vital to the ascension and healing of our planet as a whole. Your unique healing journey will uncover vast wisdom about the nature of these energies and how to clear them. The wisdom attained from embarking on a journey of complete healing will provide vital understandings for personal and collective ascension. The healing journey you undertake is the key itself. That wisdom and the sharing of the wisdom is the treasure you unlock with your key. So, this meditation introduces very subtly the deep understanding of the intention and purpose behind the fear- and separation-based energies that exist in your field.

For this meditation, it is enough to understand that you have, through the power of your voice, the unlimited capacity to heal yourself of anything that is not of a Christed nature. Furthermore, through this meditation you will also be granted inviolable protection by the light realms so that fear-based energies can no longer enter your field. This understanding will make you bold and determined in confronting these energies when you encounter them in the future.

In completing this meditation, you will set in motion purification energies that will continue to work with you until the intention you declared has been fulfilled. As you emerge from this meditation, listen deeply to your inner guidance. It will help you to become an investigator of your own life as you apply the power of your discernment to your daily choices. As you approach your life with inquiry, curiosity, and non-judgment, you will be guided, like a flower opening to the sun, toward the choices, people, and contexts that bring you into the light.

The Forces of Light

You may not have known that you are "the commander" of vast, unlimited forces of Light Beings. You may not have known that you can call on them to witness your prayers, hold space for your declarations, and ensure that your divine will is done. They are all dimensions of your all-powerful Self, and they are here to serve you. You can ask for anything, and if it is in alignment with your Higher Self, it will be granted.

As you form relationships with the divine guardians of this Passage, you will understand their specific frequencies and powers. As you do so, you can begin to call on them more and more, enacting your divine free will. This meditation shows you just a small part of what they, and therefore you – are capable of. You may not have known that you can ask for an inviolable seal of protection or deep energy clearing for the planet. You will learn more and more that when your free will is consecrated to the Divine Mind, you have unlimited power to command resources to create healing and restoration.

The Power of Intention and Prayer

This meditation offers to you, with open hands, a new way to pray. It demonstrates that when you lift your voice with pure intention and pure heart, you are held and heard by the divine.

It may be hard to believe at first, but when you speak your intention from your deepest heart, your will is done. You can trust that the Divine will take care of it. If there is more that you need to do or know, you will be alerted to it. Until then, simply trust – Miracle Consciousness and Divine Intelligence operate in ways that are breath-taking, astonishing, and unexpected. Ask, and then allow the higher realms to take care of your request in their own, divine way.

Healing and Forgiving

This meditation guides you to forgive all you have been holding that no longer serves you or creation. You will be guided to forgive the energies, the people, or beings who have brought those energies to you. You will also be guided to forgive yourself. Forgiveness is a process of letting go. It is a process of reclaiming your right to choose what belongs in the sacred temple of your life.

You may find this process challenging. No matter what arises in you, remember that the Divine Mother is always there to hold you in her soft and loving field. She is always available to help you through whatever comes up.

The Diamond from El Morya

This meditation brings another gift for you! From El Morya, you will receive a glittering diamond. El Morya represents the godly attributes of courage, certainty, power, forthrightness, self-reliance, dependability, faith and initiative. These are the qualities of the Father Principle – the statesman, the executive, the leader. As a leader, he was deeply in service to the Divine Consciousness. The diamond is a precious gift that is encoded with exactly the messages that you need at this time.

The gifts you are given in these meditations are deeply encoded artefacts that provide information to you about your soul's journey. Once you receive them, they are in your field and will continue working with you at all times, whether you are aware of it or not. If you cannot hear their message right away, don't worry. All is well. These gifts sometimes work on very subtle levels. Simply allow yourself to receive them, and they will do the rest.

Miracle Consciousness

In this initiation we work with the Arcturians to clear the earth of separation-based energies. The Arcturians are vastly powerful, spiritually advanced healers, who have for eons been helping humanity in its evolution. They are lovingly devoted to Gaia and to humanity. When we work with them, rapid and miraculous healing is possible on a very large scale. Indeed, they are able to pull to the surface and transmute the most negative and stubborn energies existing on earth.

Through the power of love, truly anything is possible. This is the foundation of Miracle Consciousness. Over time, as you work with the light encodings in these meditations, you will slowly release your doubt in miracles and magic. Over time, you will naturally inhabit this state of deep trust in the Divine's ability to bring about miracle after miracle in service to your highest purpose.

It can sometimes be difficult to feel the difference between what we feel, see and know on the inside, and what the outer world tells us. It can feel impossible that the outer world will ever mirror what we know to be true in our hearts. Part of our soul promise is to stay connected to our heart dreams and to know that what is in our hearts will become the material reality of the outer world. This is a creation mechanism.

The heart is an unlimited space of creation, and we know as creators that everything is possible. When we are in the space of our hearts, there is nothing we cannot do.

Sovereignty

Underlying each meditation is the heartbeat of your own sovereignty, calling you into Oneness with your True Self. Each meditation will always lead you back into the space of your own inner knowing. When you let yourself be guided only by the light of your heart, you enter the space of sovereignty.

This meditation was brought forth in a field of power and strength. It guides you to fully claim your power as a divine being. From this place of empowerment, you will decide for yourself what is really yours on this path of love.

As you wake up to this energy, it can sometimes come with painful insights that we are with people or in a surrounding that is not in accordance with our highest purpose. It is important to observe this and allow your heart to guide you forward.

We remind you that there is a community of Human Light Beings walking this same path with you. We are many. Do not hesitate to call us through the space of your heart to support you in your highest expression of Self.

Thank you for being here and be prepared to join the field of sovereignty and freedom.

With that, we will start.

Prepare yourself by breathing in,

and breathing out...

When you let yourself be guided
Only by the light of your heart,
You enter the space of sovereignty.

The Fourth Meditation

You are invited now to close your eyes, to draw a few deep breaths and to draw all the energy from the outside world to the inside, to your inner sanctuary. You will notice that your system becomes quieter and more still. Centre your attention in the space of your heart, in the Sacred Space of the Heart. And notice how the frequency in your system changes, how it shifts when you move your attention to the Sacred Space of the Heart. Allow yourself to feel the bliss of being in this most sacred Inner Temple, a temple that is always there and that you can enter any time you wish. And from this space, connect to Mother Earth and to Father Sky, in your own way, sending gratitude and love for your life and everything that life brings you.

Feel how Mother Earth and Father Sky send you back their love, and how you are nourished in this field of love, this field of love where everything is possible.

And slowly, gently, with a soft inner voice, start to call on the Blue Flame, the Sacred Blue Flame of Divine Love and Will. Ask that it become active in your system and in the greater Light Network, in the network of all human beings moving through the Great Passage on Earth.

And through the action of the Blue Flame, we will travel to the Temple of Divine Will and Love in India, in Darjeeling, which is a space that holds energies that support enlightened global governance, governance anchored in Divine Intelligence. You are invited to connect to this temple now.

Allow yourself to see, sense or feel this temple and the wisdom it offers you at this time through the Blue Flame. It is in this temple that you can most easily reconnect with the will of your Higher Self and to the grace that accompanies you when you follow the path of Divine Love and Will.

When you feel you have fully arrived at this temple, the master of this temple comes forward. This is Master El Morya. He greets you, heart to heart, and he offers you a diamond. This diamond has many encodings. It serves to reconnect you to your highest path, to the path of your soul, to the path of the Divine Diamond Heart.

What is it that you need to know about your path at this time?

Allow yourself to feel, sense or see the information that is coming to you at this moment. This is the Divine Guidance of your Higher Self.

You are fully supported by the Blue Flame and all the Light Beings that are holding space for you at this moment.

And while staying connected to this diamond, call on Mother Divine to dissolve all your fears and to remove any external control mechanism that might interfere with this work. Ask your Higher Self to establish crystalline channels for healing purposes, so that only Christed energies can flow to you. This channel can be used ONLY for the flow of energies originating in unconditional love.

See, sense or feel a clockwise rotation of blue energy from within your body and all around you. This rotational energy will continue for several hours.

Now call upon Archangel Michael, of the highest dimension, to completely seal and protect this sacred experience. Ask the intelligence of the ultimate dimension to remove anything that is not of a Christed nature that currently exists in this field.

Ask the Pleiadians, the Ascended Masters, the Etheric Surgeons, the Arcturians, and the Christed Helpers to remove and completely dissolve all implants and their seeded energies, emotional, mental and physical parasites, entities, spiritual weapons and self-imposed, limiting thought-forms, known and unknown, from Gaia and from other places in this universe.

Allow this work, this clearing, to take place now. Surrender to all these beings that are helping you for your highest liberation, as they work on your physical body, emotional body, mental body and soul.

See, sense or feel as the energies in your system shift and change. See, sense or feel the qualities of the energies that stay, as your system becomes purified and sovereign, and as you become whole, complete.

Connect to the purified waters of your system, to your Original Blueprint, your Divine Blueprint, to what you were meant to be. It is becoming more and more apparent.

Once this is done, we call for the complete restoration and complete repair of the original energy field infused with the golden energy of the Christ Consciousness. Claim your sovereignty as a Divine Being.

I claim my sovereignty as a Divine Being! (3x)

If you feel to do so, repeat internally the following:

"I (declare your name), in this particular incarnation, revoke and renounce each and every commitment, vow, agreement and contract that no longer serves my highest purpose. I revoke these in this life, past lives, concurrent lives, in all dimensions, times, periods and locations. I now order all entities (which are related to these contracts, organizations and associations which I am now renouncing) to cease and give up and to leave my energy field now and forever and retroactively, taking their artifacts, devices and sown energies. To ensure this, I now ask the Divine Mother to witness the dissolution of all sown contracts, devices, and energies that do not honour the Sophia Christos. This includes all covenants and beings that do not honour the Sophia Christos.

I ask that the Holy Spirit bear witness to this complete liberation from all that violates the will of the Sophia Christos. So be it.

I return now to secure my connection with the Sophia Christos through the Christ Consciousness and I dedicate my entire being, my physical, mental, emotional and spiritual being, to the vibration of the Christed Sophia. More so, I dedicate my life, my work, everything I think, say and do, and all the things in my environment that still serve me, to the vibration of the Christed Sophia.

In addition, I dedicate my being to my own mastery and to the path of ascension. Having declared all of this, I now authorize the Christ Consciousness of my Higher Self to make changes in my life to accommodate this internal direction and I ask the Holy Spirit to witness this."

Now allow for the healing and forgiveness of all aspects that made the agreements and all of those that participated in limitation in this way.

Please include in this prayer of forgiveness whoever you need to consciously forgive, as well as those who are unknown to you:

"I proclaim to the universe, to the entire Mind of God, and to every being contained in it, wherever I have been, experiences in which I have participated, and to all beings who need this healing, whether they are known or unknown to me:

I HEAL AND I FORGIVE. (3x)

I now appeal to the Holy Sophia Christos, Lord Metatron, Lord Maitreya and Saint Germain to help and witness this healing.

I forgive myself for anything that needs to be forgiven. I let go of anything that makes my heart heavy. I have fully forgiven and I am fully forgiven. I am healed and forgiven. I allow my heart to be as light as a feather."

You are now healed and forgiven, healed and forgiven, healed and forgiven. You are fully surrounded by the golden love of the Sophia Christos. You are fully surrounded by the Golden Light and Love of the Sophia Christos.

You are free from all third and fourth dimensional vibrations of fear, pain, and anger. All the chords and psychic links attached to these entities, deployed devices, contracts or energies sown, are now released and healed.

Now ask Saint Germain to transmute and rectify with the Violet Flame all energies that have been taken from you and to return them to you now in their purified state.

Once these energies have been returned to you, ask that the channels drawing out this energy be completely dissolved. Ask Lord Metatron to free you completely from the chains of duality. Ask the Holy Spirit to witness that this is happening.

And so it is.

Now ask Mary Magdalene and Yeshua to come to you, to heal your wounds and your scars, so that you can come back to your Original Divine State. Also ask Archangel Michael to protect you forever from the influences that prevent you from following the will of your inner Divine Creator Force, which is innately connected to the Natural Laws.

So be it!

Give thanks to God, to the Ascended Masters, to the Angels and Archangels, and to all who have participated in this healing and continued upliftment of your being.

Sit in silence and peace for a few more moments while the Etheric Surgeons attend to you, helping you on this incredible path of ascension. Thank the Etheric Surgeons who are tending to you and who will continue to work on your system to liberate you further.

There is protection built against re-implantation, in part because once you have completely revoked the vows, your agency and desire to remain free from implants and spiritual limitation devices will prevent you from being targeted again.

You are protected by the Galactic Federation of Light and by the Angelic Realms, and there is a wide protective belt around your energy field that moves with you throughout your day.

The Sophia Christos field has become very strong. Feel, sense or see this pulsating field of Golden Solar Light that deeply illuminates and unifies your field. With your intention, feed this frequency strongly into the Christ grid of the earth. See, sense, or feel as this quality amplifies across the earth plane, as this Sophia Christos field illuminates Gaia.

And from this Sophia Christ field, from this Golden Solar Light, we observe the Arcturian healers, the ones who have the greatest capacity to remove the strongest control forces from our earth plane. We witness them working on energy centres around the earth. They know where to go and what to do, but they need you, and others like you, to consciously hold space for them, as they create high frequency vortices in specific areas around the globe. You can witness as they put these vortices into place, and as they activate them. You may be guided to witness one in particular, or perhaps several.

Once installed, these light vortices begin to spin at an extremely high frequency, pulling out any energies still operating underground or above ground, against the freewill of humanity on Gaia. The Arcturians take these beings back to the Great Central Sun, for the benefit of all creation, so just hold space and witness as they do this work for the liberation of humanity.

As they do their work, stay in the Sacred Space of your Heart, holding the golden energy of the Christ Light. Witness how you are ONE with all the other human beings making this Great Passage.

You may feel how the frequency changes, how the reality here becomes less dense. You may feel that all of a sudden there is more space.

What is it that you are witnessing at this time, as the Arcturian healers work?

Where are you called to go? What are you called to witness?

How does your heart feel?

And now allow the Arcturians to continue their work of service, as they will continue for several more hours.

Bow to them in gratitude for their service to humanity. They have been supporting and guiding us for eons and you are finally able to be conscious of their ever-loving help. With infinite gratitude, acknowledge their support to help you ascend to higher levels of consciousness.

Now bring your consciousness back to the Temple of Divine Love and Will, in India, remaining there for a few more moments, reconnecting to the Blue Flame and to the diamond you received from El Morya.

Is there a message there for you at this time? Are you called to a certain direction? What is the next step on your Path of Love?

See, sense or feel this Temple of Divine Will and Love, and know that you can return here anytime you wish.

Slowly now, return back to your inner space with the diamond. And then slowly start to bring your awareness to the outer world, to the room where you are sitting. Gently move your fingers and your toes. Take a few deep breaths, stretch your arms and your legs, and when you are ready, open your eyes.

Thank you for this journey together.

Namaste

When you lift your voice with pure intention,

You are held and heard by the divine.

The Fifth Meditation: The Temple of Unconditional Love

Teachings of the Fifth Meditation

Welcome to the fifth meditation. This meditation was brought forth from a field of abundance and newness. In this meditation you will be initiated into the frequency of the New Earth. Congratulations! We have arrived on the shores of the New Earth together.

The Frequency of the New Earth

This meditation invites you into a new life. You are emerging now after having been purified of all of the energies that were not of the New Earth. The New Earth is dawning within you now. This newness will be unlike anything you have ever experienced. It is very tender, like a plant that has just begun to sprout, or a newly born child that has just drawn its first breath.

As a parent tenderly watches each tiny wriggle of their new born child, from the very beginning of this meditation you will be invited to simply observe yourself tenderly in your new state of being. This is a gentle and miraculous time of discovery. It is time to care for all of your precious energies. Starting with observing your breath, this meditation takes you back to your most natural actions when you yourself were just born. It reminds you to be gentle on yourself as you adjust to your new state of being.

The frequency of the New Earth is unconditional love and gratitude. You are in the process of being cleared of all things that have prevented you from giving and receiving love. The space that is opening within you after your deep purification is being filled with Christed Light. Let yourself be filled with unconditional love for your miraculous, precious Self. Throughout this meditation, the frequency of love will be transmitted to you through the encodings of the Ruby Rose and the Threefold Flame.

Like a newborn baby opening its eyes for the first time, encountering the vast world of unconditional love can feel overwhelming. You will awaken gently into this frequency in the safe environment of the Temple of Unconditional Love. You will awaken there, surrounded by loving Beings of Light who will carefully and gently midwife you into the New Earth. They will be with you until these frequencies have stabilized in your being, no matter how long that takes.

Observing Triggers

It is possible that, after this meditation, you will feel very tender. The barriers that were removed in the third meditation previously kept you from receiving love, and they also kept you in a state of relative numbness towards the outside world. Now those barriers are being cleansed, and you may feel the world bursting in on your senses in a new way. It will be very important for you to stay as much as possible in peaceful spaces, for as long as you need to adjust. Allow yourself as much time as you need. Allow yourself to gravitate naturally toward that which is nourishing, loving, and safe. Use the power of your "no" to remove that which feels painful or heavy from your life.

So, we invite you to observe your triggers in the coming days. You may feel that your emotions, and even physical sensations, are amplified in response to anything and anyone who is not coming from a place of love. This is a very normal and natural response to awakening out of a state of numbness. Observe your response, listen to what it is trying to tell you, and allow yourself to be held in this temple, full of consolation and compassion. Remember that the Divine Mother is always with you.

The frequency of the New Earth is one of naturalness and transparency. We invite you to enjoy this exciting time of discovery as you start to see what comes naturally to you when you are totally free. Watch yourself with love and tenderness, as though discovering yourself for the first time. How does your body like to move? What do you like to eat? What feels good and nourishing and relaxing to you? What environments suit you best? Allow yourself to gravitate toward those things. Observe what is true for you in this new place of freedom and unconditional love. We invite you also to record or journal on what you observe about yourself in this potent time of rebirth and re-discovery.

We want to add that your commitment to this inner work is truly transforming the world. It may feel selfish or indulgent to spend so much time investigating and caring for the Self. We want to reassure you that this is the most important work you can be doing at the moment because the outer world is changed by changing the inner world. Through your active discipline and engagement, by being present and standing up, in committing to join your heart with this global community of brothers and sisters of the Light, the whole New Earth is really and truly moving in the direction that we have been praying for. Love yourself, care for yourself, and trust that these simple acts have the power to transform the world.

The Body and Mind

At this time in the Passage it is important to tend deeply to your inner realms. It is here that you will find the voice of your heart. We are halfway through the initiations of this Passage, and we are moving very deeply into a space where the outer world makes less and less sense for the mind. The terrain you are entering is unmapped, and only your heart can guide you through it. The field in which this meditation was brought forth was one of plenitude and potential, but also darkness. It is the darkness of the womb. This meditation was brought forth in the very middle of December, when the very last rose was cut from the bush.

We invite you, then, to take time in silence and reflection. Allow the stories and cords of the outside world to fall away so that you can integrate all that the New World has to offer. Be in nature.

Tend carefully and gently to your body at this time. Listen to its needs and nurture yourself.

Inner Guidance

These meditations have come to awaken deep wisdom and memories within you. We say once again that the most important thing in this Passage is for you to trust in your experiences. When you meet unknown guides or travel to these unmapped temples, you are invited to form your own relationship with them regardless of what you have read or been taught.

When you feel resonance, this is confirmation that a teaching or a Light Being has something to offer you at this time. We want to note that you may feel a deep resonance arising underneath resistance. Only your Higher Self can tell you if the resistance is from your ego or from your soul. If you suspect there is a message for you underneath your resistance, you can always ask that the guidance you need, be delivered in a way that is gentler or more natural for you.

If there is no resonance at all, it simply means that an information or teaching is not for you at this point in time. This Passage is not an intellectual exercise, but a soulful, experiential journey of the heart. If you find yourself caught in the conflict of the mind, relax and let the answer come to you through the heart. When you are in the space of the heart, you will connect with the beings and experiences in exactly the way that is right for you.

Freedom

In the last meditation you were set free from all that is not serving your highest purpose. This experience of freedom will continue to unfold for you as you stretch into the vast space you have opened within your life.

The freedom you experience in this meditation may arise in you as a pure state of being. This means that you belong fully to yourself. You are not controlled or owned by anyone or anything. We invite you to expand into the infinite potential and power of freedom. This is the beginning of a vast exploration for you!

The Threefold Flame: Rubies and Gold

You will notice a strong theme of fire and flames moving through this meditation. Flames are alchemical. They are connected to the dragon and the phoenix and they signal a rebirth. Specifically, you will receive the gift of the awesome, transformative Threefold Flame.

Let yourself be showered by treasures in this meditation, treasures of ruby and gold, colours and frequencies that twine through this journey. You will be given a ruby sphere of unconditional love from the hands of Mary Magdalene herself, and you will also be given a ruby rose. Both of these ruby gifts hold the frequency of the New Earth. As you receive them into your heart, you will feel the frequency of unconditional love.

You will also receive gold, a precious, alchemical frequency. When you are in the Temple of Unconditional Love, golden droplets and rays will shower onto you from the Great Central Sun. This is the solar, masculine element that will mix with the divine feminine of the ruby frequency, as overseen by the Holy Spirit. Your consciousness, as it is fertilized by these masculine and feminine elements, is being subtly prepared for Oneness Consciousness. Let these alchemical frequencies sing through your blood and ignite your Light Body. Observe what happens in your bodies as these energies come together inside of you.

It is here, in the Sacred Space of the Heart, that we can see the significance of the Threefold Flame. It burns bright as the Holy Trinity within. The feminine ruby flame, the masculine golden flame, and the ineffable final flame – Holy Spirit – all in one. Relax and receive this powerful, alchemical gift. Let it set in motion a merging with your highest divine expression.

It is now time to move into meditation and receive these gifts of the beautiful New Earth. We invite you to prepare your space and your body by becoming still and silent. Prepare yourself in any way that is sacred and loving.

Breathe in, and breathe out.

It is time to begin.

We trust the divine hand
That is guiding us all
Toward our own
Inevitable blossoming.

The Fifth Meditation

Make yourself comfortable, in a way that is best for you. You might want to sit up straight or you may prefer to lie down. Make sure that your spine is straight from top to bottom, but do not force anything. Be gentle on your body. Feel that from the inside of your body, there is an active presence.

And when you find the right position, one that is comfortable for you, bring your attention to your breath. Feel a velvet stream of air coming into your body and giving you all you need. Observe also how the exhalation of air moves through, and out of, your body. Just observe the rhythm of your breath without changing anything. Just observe. It is perfect the way it is, and it is the most natural thing that you have been doing since you were born. Breathe in and breathe out.

Be aware that this air is filled with prana, with particles of energy that are nourishing your body, and are connecting you to all life on Gaia. Observe yourself for a moment. Observe how you feel in this moment. Just observe. See and remember all the gifts that you have been given in your life to arrive in this moment.

And feel the gratitude inside of you growing – for the gift of transformation; for the gift of insight; for the gift of love; and for the gift of connection. So many gifts have come your way, sometimes through very dense and difficult moments in life. All these experiences have been there to provide you gifts in life.

So take a moment to observe the gifts that have been given to you. And even if it is difficult for you to find them, they can be in the tiniest things in your life – the connection to another living being, which can be an animal, or a plant, or a tree. These gifts can be in anything.

And when you feel to do so, say thank you for all these gifts that you have received. Bring this deep gratitude into your network of Light now, and to all the loved ones in your life. You have come here to stand up for a world anchored in love and light; a new world based in harmony and peace. Bring this intense feeling of gratefulness to all those around you, to all Human Light Beings, who together form a family that stands for the same values. You, and so many others, have the same vision of an earth in perfect harmony, where all living beings live in peace.

In expressing this gratitude, feel how the deep connection with your soul family intensifies, and feel the unity with the hearts of all the people in this network. See them, feel the desire for loving connection, and feel a deepening presence of love and light on Gaia. You are connected to fellow travellers from all around the world. Envision all these Beacons of Light, all across Gaia, holding the Light, holding this very strong fabric of Love & Light, because you have all received this solar light, this intelligence. Hold this solar light in your heart as a flame of love.

And when you bring your attention to your heart space, see that inside of your heart, there is this Eternal Flame of Love. It is always present. It is always there. It is a flame of freedom.

Now, along with your fellow travellers, you are invited to slowly move to the most beautiful sanctuary in nature, to a sanctuary called the Temple of Unconditional Love. It is a place to find consolation and comfort. It is an etheric sanctuary where a crystal rose, a high frequency crystal rose, is waiting for you.

Move to this sanctuary, where you are welcomed by the ascended master Paul the Venetian, who is holding the Flame of Unconditional Love for you. He is with Mary Magdalene and Yeshua, in front of the Temple of Unconditional Love. You are invited to find a place for yourself in this sanctuary. Take your time to connect to this sacred place. Find a comfortable place, either inside or outside.

This place is held by the Ruby Rose Flame, which is connected to deep love. You might even smell the fragrance of the rose, because the whole place is filled with the frequency of the ruby rose. It is here for you. Today you are invited to understand the deeper meaning of love as an eternal presence.

So as you find a comfortable place for yourself in this sanctuary, you may find yourself in nature, but still inside this etheric temple. Find the perfect place for you, a place that you are drawn to. Feel how this whole place is filled with eternal love and the most perfect harmony. It is peaceful and the whole sanctuary is held in a space of silence.

When you have found your place, make yourself comfortable there and prepare yourself to meet Mary Magdalene. She comes towards you to offer you a most sacred ruby sphere of energy. Hold up your hands and receive this ruby sphere. Mary Magdalene smiles at you with the most loving eyes, providing you with a feeling of deep comfort.

While you hold this sphere of ruby energy, and feel this nourishing, warm, loving energy flow inside of you, witness how it fills your whole body. This is the frequency of universal love that is ever present, everywhere. Take a few moments to fully take this energy in. You might want to breathe it in, you might want to lie down in it, or you might want to sit in it. Just let it fill your whole physical body and all your subtle bodies. Let it fill you and activate you with the memory of love.

See, sense or feel that Mary Magdalene is still with you, guiding this sacred process inside of you. And in so doing, she aligns you with the Divine Mother, the Creator, and with the Sophia Universal Wisdom.

You don't have to do anything, just allow it to happen. Be ready to be of service.

Now bring your attention to the sky above you. See, sense or feel that golden drops from the sun are falling all over you. These are photonic light particles. From within your now ruby presence, allow these drops to fuse with your body, to fill you with a divine golden glow, full of divine intelligence. See that these golden drops can also turn into rays, and they fill your ruby body with a golden inner shimmer.

Just observe – be present and observe. There is nothing for you to do, just allow these particles to come into your system.

You can feel the presence of Yeshua becoming stronger and stronger. It is now time for you to ask that the full memory of your divine destiny be unveiled. When you are ready, ask that this memory of your divine destiny rise to the surface. This can come in words, in forms or shapes, as a knowingness, or in any other way. Just let it arise, nothing else. And if there is nothing there for you today, just continue to hold space, in observation.

Stay in this field of unconditional love and light and feel how the universal intelligence takes care of itself, in you and through you. This sanctuary is held by Paul the Venetian, and holds the remembrance of the Holy Spirit. You may experience an intense flow of life from Source. Stay open.

The flow of golden light continues to stream in, and it will do so for the coming days.

When you look inside of your heart, you will now find a Threefold Flame made of ruby, gold and Holy Spirit. See, sense or feel this Threefold Flame in your heart. And see that with your attention and intention you can make it grow. From a small flame, you can make a large flame that radiates a ruby-gold energy into your whole surroundings.

So, see what you can do with your Threefold Flame to expand it. Flood your whole surroundings with this gift. Flood the people

around you and all living beings with the ruby-gold universal
Love & Light. Share your Threefold Flame unconditionally. You
might want to make it even bigger, so it encompasses the village,
town, or city you live in, then your region, and your country.
You might want to envelop the whole planet and even beyond. It
is an infinite source, so it can be as big as you feel you want to
make it.

See, sense, feel or know that this flame is encoded with the
protection of the Divine Mother of Freedom, who is in the soul
of this flame. The love and the wisdom inside of this creator-
flame are holding the intelligence for a New Earth of harmony
and peace.

Now observe yourself. Bring your energy back to yourself and
see that YOU ARE this flame. You ARE this flame of freedom.
You ARE this ruby-gold flame. And you hold its wisdom
and you hold its love. You ARE the Light. All of your fellow
travellers also hold this Light.

Observe that you have now returned to the Temple of
Unconditional Love, to this sanctuary of comfort and
consolation. If you feel that anyone in your environment needs
consolation at this time, now is the time to invite them into the
temple, to be held in this field of unconditional love. Invite those
who you feel should be invited into the Temple of Unconditional
Love. Observe how they are cared for by the Light Beings that
hold the rose.

Hold space for this sacred moment of deep loving consolation
that leads to freedom. Observe how the circle of Light Beings
becomes stronger and stronger. See, sense or feel the arrival of
the Ascended Masters. Together, you will make one big circle
with them in this sanctuary. In the centre, you can see Mary
Magdalene and Yeshua. You can observe how the Holy Spirit
moves through them and with them. You can also feel their
eternal connection to Source, Eternal Creation, to Creator.

You are gifted with so much love! Feel the flow of love and the embrace of consolation for all the experiences on Gaia that need consolation and comfort. Feel how all is cared for, and dissolves in the source of love. See or feel the presence of the Holy Family.

Now it is time for you to receive a ruby rose from one of the Light Beings. This is the Ruby Rose of the New Earth. You are invited to take the ruby rose and bring it inside of your heart, into the Threefold Flame. You might want to put your hands on your heart and feel the presence of this rose of unconditional love. It is inside of you, it IS you. Observe how you fuse together with this rose. Feel your gratitude for this gift of love that you are able to receive in this Eternal Now moment.

In this deep state of love, a prayer may arise from inside of your heart, a prayer for the highest good of all of life. If such a prayer arises, you are invited to speak it out, to give it to the world. You might want to use your voice for toning or humming to accompany your prayer. Your heart prayer may be with words, but it could also be without words. Hold this prayer in your heart for the coming week.

You continue the Great Passage with an ever-deepening understanding of Love & Light. You are in deep connection with your freedom, your ever-present inner freedom.

Now hold the rose and the prayer inside of your heart, together with the Threefold Flame, while you make yourself ready to give thanks to all the ascended beings that have come to accompany you in this sacred sanctuary. Thank them and honour them for their presence and service to humanity. You know you can always come back to this beautiful temple to nourish yourself, to fill yourself with Light and Love, and to remind yourself of the eternal source of love, the Light of the Sophia Christos.

Thank Paul the Venetian from the bottom of your heart, for being present on this planet in many moments, in many timelines. Thank him for reminding you of your freedom, for reminding you that you are a sovereign being. Thank him deeply for that reminder.

Honour and thank Mary Magdalene and her beloved Yeshua, who together are One, for sharing their presence, their love, light and unity today in this channel. Thank them for the gift of this grace. So much grace is coming your way, and so much grace already exists within you!

Thank all the Light Beings and the Ascended Masters in the temple, and then prepare yourself to bring your attention back to the place where you are sitting or lying. Observe your heart space for a few moments, with your eyes closed. Feel the quietness, coming from the remembrance of the space of oneness within you. Feel this silence from the depth of your heart, and feel how it is the basis of your body. Remember that this stillness and tranquillity is always there, even when it is noisy in the outside world. This peace is an eternal peace that comes from the awareness of your inner spaciousness. So, enjoy this spaciousness and silence.

Then bring your attention back to your breathing, and feel how your body is made of the rhythm of your breath and the rhythm of your heartbeat. Thank your physical body for being there for you, so that you can experience Gaia's magical paradise.

Hold your attention on your body for a moment, giving it gratitude that it is always there for you, no matter how you are doing. Your body is your best friend, your personal Earth Temple, your real home on Gaia. Give it lots and lots of love.

And slowly start moving, moving your hands, your fingers, and your toes. You can give yourself a light massage, just to bring all your awareness back to your physical temple. Maybe you feel like touching your face, or your legs. Keep your eyes closed, and stay inwardly focused. Maybe you want to stretch a little bit. But all the time stay connected to the silence and to the Threefold Flame in your heart. And remember the rose.

When you are ready, but take your time, open your eyes. Continue to feel the flame and the rose inside of you. Stay a little while in this place to feel that you have fully come back to your body. And only when you feel that you are ready, then begin to think about your day. Stay as long as you like in the internal silence, and in the preciousness of this moment.

You can do this meditation anytime to align your frequency with that of the New Earth. You can visit the Temple of Unconditional Love at any moment, and its guardians will always welcome you, whenever you need comfort and consolation.

Have a blessed day!

Namaste

The Sixth Meditation:
The Tiny Space of the Heart

Teachings of the Sixth Meditation

Welcome to the sixth meditation of your Sacred Passage.

This meditation was brought forth in a field of lightness and joy. Two hours before it was shared by the spoken word to soul family all over the globe, Saturn had moved fully into Aquarius. The meditation holds the frequency of that auspicious moment. It heralds in your life a message of something completely new coming into form.

Allow yourself to feel the potency and anticipation of this moment. You have received the blueprint of the New Earth; with this meditation we prepare to build from it with aligned direction and purpose.

The Tiny Space of the Heart

We would like to introduce this meditation with a short metaphor.

In the Zen tradition there is a practice known as a "walking meditation." In this practice, a person will move their foot two or three inches, and then pause. They will then move the other foot two or three inches, and then pause. In ten minutes they may have moved only a few feet.

This sixth meditation is very like that Zen practice. In the previous few journeys we have followed a rhythm where, through the Sacred Space of the Heart, you have travelled to etheric temples on Gaia. Slowly, gently, and with great wonder, these meditations have been showing you how to move, in your etheric body, on guided adventures in the inner planes. These journeys offered a sensory feast: visions and gifts, bright colours, frequencies, and Light Beings to welcome and care for you.

You will notice a very different quality to this meditation. If you attempt to understand it from what we have done so far, you will not receive its full benefit. Like the Zen monk who moves but has no destination, you will not actually go anywhere in this meditation. The point of this journey is not to travel, but to move simply into a place of inner stillness, an empty space of unlimited potential.

In this meditation, you will be introduced, not to another etheric temple on Gaia, but to a holy temple deep, deep inside of you. This temple is one that you have perhaps never accessed before. It is called the Tiny Space of the Heart, and it is the centre of the whole universe. Coming into this space is an indicator that you have come a long way on your path of illumination, for the Tiny Space of the Heart has been an extremely protected secret for millennia. When you enter it, you can create anything immediately. In times of darkness and forgetting, this access point to Creation was hidden by the veils. It can only be entered with a pure and willing heart.

The Tiny Space of the Heart is a place of pure presence. You have consecrated yourself to the New Earth, and now it is time to go within and discover what that means for your life. To do this, you will access the part of you that is, and has always been, completely free from the constructs of the current world. This part of you is the Tiny Space of the Heart. From here, all that is not truth will wash away. From this place of pure stillness, something completely new can be born within you.

You will notice long periods of silence in this meditation. Let the silence be velvety and welcoming. Sink into it, as you would a soft embrace of loam and moss from your Divine Mother. As you relax and breathe into the deep void of the Self, simply allow what wants to arise. It will come from the deeps. Gently, it will break the surface of the waters of your heart. Allow the emergence of this miracle, arising from the depths of your wondrous heart.

Sacred Responsibility

From this space of stillness, you will receive the message of your sacred responsibility. This is the blueprint for your new way of life in the New Earth. The message of your sacred responsibility is the higher, expanded Saturn energy rising within you: the energy of structure, direction, and discipline that stems from actualising your complete freedom and sovereignty. Discipline is not anything to resist, but a practice of freedom and balance. Feel the message of your responsibility alight in your awareness. It is bracing and invigorating: a splash of lemon in your water, a brisk walk on a clear autumn day, delightful, gentle sandpaper brush of the skin. Let it rouse your senses and bring the blood to hum with life in your veins.

This sacred responsibility is a promise you made to yourself. It is a pathway to your deepest fulfilment, your highest expression. It arises from the sparkling blueprint of your soul. This responsibility is the vow of your Higher Self, the purpose of your existence. It is the only vow left after the deep process of clearing and purification of the previous meditations.

However, as you absorb the essence of this meditation, you will understand that your sacred responsibility is not something you can do. It is simply what you are. Your sacred responsibility is the unique way in which you embody the New Earth. Indeed, when you step into a pure state of sovereignty, "doing" and "being" meld together, merging as one and the same.

When we receive the message of our sacred responsibility, we see how, seamlessly, our deepest fulfilment and joy is connected to the good of all beings. We can embrace our responsibility unreservedly, knowing that the happiness of our deepest being enhances the happiness of all.

As your sacred responsibility is revealed to you, you will feel a deep and abiding YES in your heart, even if a part of you has difficulty believing in it. Most likely, what will be shown to you will not come from constructs known in the current world. As you return to this meditation again and again, the message of your purpose will mature, clarifying itself into a diamond of inexpressible magic. Right now it is enough to allow yourself to be introduced to it in whatever form it chooses to arise.

This meditation hints at a larger teaching that will reveal itself more fully in later volumes. This later teaching explores how, in the New Earth, we will naturally create new roles for ourselves – ones that are tailored to our precise purpose. These roles exist far beyond what our current concepts and constructs can possibly imagine. We joke that the new roles coming to earth will look very funny when they're written on business cards!

So, with that wide expanse of possibility as your context, allow your sacred responsibility to come to you. Open yourself to it in whatever form it chooses to appear. Even if it looks or feels strange at first, even if you don't have a framework or a language for it, whatever it is will resonate deeply in your heart. Simply allow it and trust what arises as you go within.

The Solar Principle

You are the Holy Child of Earth and Sky. Your heart is the centre of the Holy Trinity. In this meditation you will use your body to bridge the ineffable space between Earth and Sun, Mother and Father. Your heart will become the centre-point between, and you will embody each of them fully as you have been designed to do since your conception.

You will then travel briefly to the sun to receive a gift from your Heavenly Father. The Sun, our solar masculine, fertilizes the seeds of your heart-dreams so that they can grow in your life. Allow yourself to be bathed in this vital, solar light. You will then return to the Tiny Space of the Heart carrying the frequency of creation, fertilization and light, to help manifest your sacred purpose on Gaia.

Through this simple practice you begin to see yourself as the natural, holy bridge between formlessness and form. As you work with this meditation, you will emerge with the blessing of fulfilment and confidence, able to move through the world clearer about your purpose on this earth and your sovereign ability to manifest it.

Surrender

We would like to end this teaching with a deep breath of contentment. Trust that everything has already been done. The seeds have already been planted and are ready to grow. This is a space of surrender, of trust. There is nothing to worry about and nothing to do. Let your worries fall away. All is accounted for and cared for. Let yourself revel in the simple things around you. Notice the abundance that lives in simplicity.

Breathe in

And breathe out.

It is time to begin.

The Sixth Meditation

You are invited to make yourself comfortable, either sitting or lying down. Close your eyes and draw a few deep breaths. Slowly bring your awareness into your inner space, your inner temple. And with each breath, feel how your system begins to relax more and more. Let go of what is unnecessary and become more and more relaxed. Feel the weight of gravity as you do so. Feel how good it is to just BE here and now, in the present moment. Nothing exists aside from this present moment.

And slowly, in your own way, connect with Mother Earth and Father Sky. Thank them, send them your love and your gratitude for this opportunity to be here, to experience life as it is now. Give thanks for the multitude of adventures you have lived, for this dream that you are participating in. Give thanks for the changes, for the transformations, for this gift of consciousness, for this gift of eternal life.

And when you feel both the energies of Mother Earth and Father Sky in your heart space, just feel that blend of energies, that alchemy of love.

Then, slowly move into the Sacred Space of the Heart. If you already know how to move into this sacred space, then please do so.

If you are new to this, just bring your awareness to the back of your physical heart. There, you will see a vortex. All you need to do is to step into this vortex and it will pull you through into the Sacred Space of the Heart.

So place yourself behind your heart, your physical heart, look for the vortex, and just step into it and allow yourself to be pulled through to the Sacred Space of the Heart.

When you arrive in the Sacred Space of the Heart, allow the lights to go on if they are not on already. And just see, sense or feel what it is like to be in this beautiful sacred temple. This is your Inner Temple. It is yours and you can come here any time you wish, to spend a few moments feeling this space and sensing its sacredness.

You may see colours, or people you know or do not know. You may see people who are special to you on your path, on your life journey. You may see images of events, or sense presences that are perhaps new. Your whole life journey can be accessed in this most sacred space. Spend a few minutes here, to imbue yourself with this vibration.

And now, you are going to move into the Tiny Space of the Heart. Do this simply through intention. This is your inner toroidal field. You can move there any way you wish, it makes no difference. And it may look various ways when you get there. You may end up in a cave, or in the stars. It may be dark, even though it is filled with light.

Allow yourself to settle into the stillness of this space. You will feel yourself being absolutely still. This is the Holiest of Holies, the most sacred space in all of the universe.

When you have become completely still, allow the light to come into your field of vision. And if you are still moving, keep going until you feel yourself stopping. You may find water in this tiny space. Whatever it is that you see, allow yourself a moment to approach it. Follow your intuition. Trust yourself completely in this space. Allow the process to unravel on its own.

Allow yourself to rest totally and completely in this great, vast stillness. Feel the expansiveness of this serenity.

And feel how wonderful it is for the heart to be in this tranquillity – to allow, to give over, to surrender.

And feel how this stillness nourishes you at the deepest levels of your being. Continue to explore this space, not actively, but through allowance, through revelation.

You are One with the Heart of the Universe. Your hearts beats as One.

This is the field of the One Heart, where all life in the universe is connected, in the greatest stillness.

This is a space where you allow things to happen organically. There is no analysis, just allowance. There is pure beingness. Spend a few minutes here to feel how it is...

And without losing contact with this space, stretch your left hand into the centre of Gaia, to the core-centre, to the diamond light inside the earth. Touch that light with your left hand. Expand your arm all the way into the Inner Earth. Connect with this light and feel this light in your left hand.

And then, your right hand is going to stretch all the way to the centre of our sun, making contact with the core of our sun. The right hand feels this amazing light of the sun, while the left hand is feeling the amazing light of Gaia. You will hold these two energies in your hands for just a moment. Allow yourself to be nourished by these two energies. Allow these two energies to fuse with your hands.

And when your hands have been fully infused, bring back your hands and lay them on your heart, bringing this light into your heart, infusing your heart with all of this light. You are deeply nourished from these two sources.

When your heart has been fully infused by these light sources, take your hands and move them to a place on your body that needs support at this time.

Remember that you are innocent, you are pure, and you are eternal. The universe is your home, and you are the Divine Light. You are innocent, you are pure and you are eternal. The whole universe is your home, and you are the Divine Light!

So, when this energy, this light from Gaia and the Sun, has completely infused your system, everywhere it needs to go, prepare yourself to travel into the heart of the sun, of the sun of this solar system. Just with intention, be there. And allow yourself to see, sense or feel what it is like.

And now, with your intention, move into the Heart of the Universe again, into the stillness. Move to the centre point of creation, to the space of infinite potential, where everything is possible. Allow yourself to settle again into the stillness and peace. Allow yourself to feel the whole universe within you. Everything that exists, exists within you. You are One with All. Sense this in all of the cells of your body.

From this space of infinity, feel YOUR sacred responsibility in this universe. Remember that responsibility is a gift, not a burden. Be grateful for it. What is YOUR responsibility at this time? What is your sacred task? There is no need to analyse, to search. Just allow it to be revealed. This is your greatest gift. It is your greatest joy. Allow it to reveal itself.

You may see colours, shapes or forms. It does not all have to make sense at this moment in time. Just allow the revelation to happen organically, in its own time, in its own way.

It may be a feeling; it may be an emotion. It could be absolutely anything. Allow space for what needs to be revealed, at this time.

And now, see, sense or feel yourself as a multidimensional being, in many dimensions simultaneously. What does that feel like? Is there a message for you, from this point of view?

And now, slowly come back to the space where you are sitting or lying down, slowly making contact with your environment. Listen to the sounds in your space. Feel the air touching your skin. Bring your focus back to where you are. Wiggle your fingers and your toes, and start to move your body a little bit. Feel your body in the space where you are sitting or lying down. Take a few deep breaths to come back fully into the here and now.

And when you are ready, you can slowly open your eyes.

Namaste

The Seventh Meditation:
The Temple of Unity and Peace

Teachings of the Seventh Meditation

Welcome to the seventh meditation, the second-last crystal stone on the Rainbow Bridge. This meditation was brought forth from a field of preparation and anticipation. It was shared for the first time on December 20, 2020, with the intention of it being available in the times to come. It came through on the eve of the solstice, the day before Saturn and Jupiter conjoined in their stately dance through the cosmos.

In this meditation we stand at the door of the new era, the New Earth. You are invited to step boldly up to the threshold.

Preparing Naturally

Throughout this initiation there is a very subtle teaching that lies just under the surface: let yourself do what comes naturally to you. This is all you need to know to embody the New Earth. This initiation holds the frequency of the New Earth, and the New Earth is one of naturalness. You are being guided to shed all that does not serve. In this way you can return to your most natural state, the one that exists in harmony with Gaia and all of her natural kingdoms.

Know that, as you absorb this meditation, a very strong light will be entering your body. As always, we invite you to be very gentle with yourself. Listen to your natural rhythms; slow your pace so that you can really hear the voice of your body speaking to you with its needs. Self-care will be very important for integrating with ease all that wants to come to you.

While the meditation was brought forward in a field of preparation and anticipation, the meditation itself does not require that you bring tension into your body. The words and cadence are infused with calm and joy, allowing you to relax into the shifts that are awaiting you. To prepare yourself and Gaia for this great shift requires you to do nothing more than the most natural action of your being: to simply breathe.

Light – Illumination – Enlightenment

Light! This meditation brings you Light like you have never felt it before. Prepare to shine like the dawn! As your heart's light merges with that of Gaia and the Sun, you will feel yourself becoming a beacon of light for the New Earth. This is a light never before seen on earth. It infuses your cells and breaks open your very DNA into a new, crystalline form. Breathing is the only action needed for you to take in this miraculous light. As you breathe light like air, it will spread through your body through your own steady heartbeat. The simple act of inhaling will open your body to light, and the simple act of exhaling will send it out to every being on the planet.

As you sink deeply into the natural rhythm of your breath, you will be shown a law of love that dissolves any lingering fear of scarcity or lack. As you breathe, you see that love, light, and all that is real, expands easily when it is freely given. Far from being depleted when we give, we find ourselves filled beyond measure when we share the infinite light of our heart.

The Temple Mount in Jerusalem

Prepare your shining awareness to travel to the holy Temple Mount of Jerusalem: a seat of the New Earth. Temple Mount is the home of the etheric Temple of Unity and Peace, located at an ancient portal dating to the beginning times on earth. The portal contains memories of the earth's conception and birth. It holds the innocence and purity of the earth in its most natural, paradisiacal state.

Overseeing this beautiful Temple of the New Earth are King Solomon and the Queen of Sheba. These sovereign Twin Ray aspects are keepers of ancient earthly wisdom. Together, they hold knowledge of the Universal Light that lives within Gaia's natural energy matrix. The meditation introduces us to these powerful Ascended Masters. We invite you to open yourself to their frequencies, as they have much they want to teach you.*

Gaia's Energy Body

As your Light Body is being activated, so too is Gaia's. As Gaia activates, so do you. As her precious child, you and she share the same consciousness. You are a living fractal of her being. You may receive a sense or an image of the harmonious and complex shape of Gaia's energy body as you move through this meditation. We refer to it as the "Christ grid," which is a network of sacred geometry that arches over and through her multi-dimensional being. Dotted along the grid at high-frequency points of convergence are holy places of worship. These places were erected by prior civilizations to anchor her energy in those potent places where lines of her grid crossed.

As you learn about the 144 etheric temples and the countless pyramids that have been erected, both in the physical and etheric realms, on the surface of the earth and in places that are now under the oceans, you may feel a newfound sense of awe and wonder for this planet. We are being introduced here to the understanding that Gaia is alive and awash with hidden ancient knowledge. She is much bigger, older, more enigmatic, more interconnected and more interdimensional than we may have ever realized. Only a tiny fraction of her many secrets have been revealed to us. As we uncover our personal divine blueprint, we also begin to uncover

---

*King Solomon and the Queen of Sheba are ascended masters that hold keys to the Twin Ray Consciousness and, in cooperation with Divine Will and the Universal Laws, they create a field of unity based on the original blueprint of Planet Earth. Some of their descendants continue to embody this consciousness; their lineage is still incarnated on earth and is in the process of awakening.

the complex and miraculous blueprint of our Mother Gaia. We can begin to feel our own sense of anticipation and excitement at the dawning of the New Earth, as we see that these meditations only hint at the knowledge that is to come.

Twin Ray Angels

The Twin Ray energy is very present in this meditation. As you journey in this meditation, you will meet the Rainbow Twin Ray Angels. These Angels will prepare you for the final meditation of this Passage by offering you a loving and powerful healing designed exactly for your unique needs at this time.

We encourage you not to become too focused on deciphering the Twin Ray aspect of this meditation. Simply allow yourself to receive this healing and notice what arises as you work with the wonderful Rainbow Angels, who are masters, guides and protectors of the Rainbow Consciousness.

Miracle Consciousness

This meditation invites us to embrace miracle consciousness as our new, daily reality. Indeed, after all we have suffered, our Passage into the New Earth, and our coming together in harmony, love, peace, and Sophia Christ Consciousness, marks one of the greatest miracles in the history and the herstory of humanity.

Miracle Consciousness means awakening every day to the understanding that anything, truly anything is possible when living in the New Earth: instantaneous healing, universal peace, perfect health and restoration of the planet. Anything you dream in your heart can manifest before you. In this way, we awaken into unity and connection with all of life on Earth. We begin to see, as well, how connected we are to all other miraculous beings in the universe.

The New Earth is the miracle that we are creating together. All of us in this Great Passage have been carrying a bone-deep dream of harmony and peace for a long, long time. As the New Earth dawns within us, we feel that longing and quickened sense of desire as we sense this long-held dream becoming reality. As we connect with the purity of our hearts, we remember that we truly can bring forth miracles together. This is our time to remember, to awaken, to live our soul's vow, to rise together, and to speak into existence the New Earth that is waiting to be born.

Indigenous Wisdom

We acknowledge with deep gratitude the many tribes around our planet who have carried the wisdom of this Passage through the ages. Members of these tribes are the wisdom keepers and guardians of life on earth. Some tribes have been preparing for this Passage for several thousand years, holding sacred in their hearts the knowledge of the prophecies that are now coming into being. We gratefully acknowledge them and humbly join our light with theirs.

Now, it is time to prepare yourself for this wondrous initiation by coming into the natural rhythm of your breath.

Breathe in

And breathe out...

Like a gardener of light walking the Earth,

Mary Magdalene sowed

The seeds of our resurrection

In her lifetime on Earth.

The Seventh Meditation

Prepare yourself slowly for today's miraculous journey by becoming silent. Take a few moments to arrive in this beautiful moment of connection. You are a part of a beautiful network of beings that is making this journey together.

Take time to arrive inside of yourself, and to observe yourself for a moment. Observe yourself, fully accepting where you are right now. Accept that you are the Divine You, and that you are perfect, exactly as you are meant to be. You, as you are, are part of the greater plan. You are Divine Light.

And through your Divine Light, through your deep essence, connect to all that is. Feel the flow of gratitude that is moving in all directions, from one being to another in this Great Passage. Feel this gratitude flowing between all human beings, all the Light Realms, and the Nature Kingdom. Feel how it is flowing through and between all the realms of life.

Feel how all these beings are so grateful that you have showed up now. You are so loved! And in that field of love that is building more and more, connect to the centre of your heart.

The centre of your heart is a place of eternal silence. It is a place of everlasting serenity, yet it is full of life. It is the eternal part of your heart, which will always be there. Here, you will find pure life, pure spirit. Connect to this one point of stillness. It is a point of tranquillity and spaciousness. It is a place of unity. It is your inner solar star, the guiding star of this life and beyond.

You may see it as an Inner Light that is very, very bright, with a magnificent radiance. And in this radiant place, you know that this is who you truly are. You are Eternal Divine Consciousness.

From this place of Inner Light, move your attention slowly to the centre of Gaia. From this heart space, move down into the earth, all the way to the diamond core of the earth, where you find the crystalline solar light of Gaia. Connect with that source of light, with this loving light, an ever-giving, ever-nourishing light that is full of love. And when you connect to the inner solar source of our planet, feel that there is a ray of light coming back to you. This light comes up through Gaia, through your body, all the way up to the centre of your heart.

And now connect your breath to this ray of light. When you inhale, breathe in pure photonic light from Gaia's inner solar loving light, allowing it to rise up through your body, all the way into your heart space. And then breathe it out into the earth realms, witnessing the photonic light spreading out all across the globe.

Do this a few more times. Inhale and exhale. Breathe out all of this photonic light, to nourish all living beings on Gaia – human beings, animals, plants, mineral and elementals. Allow it to nourish all the beings in the second and third dimension that are presently living on Gaia. You are connected to them all through the photonic light of Gaia.

Inhale and exhale. Send out the beautiful Love-Light connection. And perhaps you will notice that these realms respond to your gift of light. Just observe.

And now bring your attention back to the Space of the Heart. When your attention is back, move it slowly up through your body, through your crown chakra, all the way up into the sky and towards the Galactic Central Sun. When you move into the centre of the Galactic Central Sun, you will find the most radiant golden light intelligence. The moment you connect with the centre of the Galactic Sun, see, sense or feel that there is a ray of light, the solar light of the Heavenly Father, travelling back towards you, all the way down to your body.

It arrives in your body through your crown chakra, and moves down into the space of your heart, where it joins the light of Gaia.

See, sense or feel the streaming photonic light from the Galactic Central Sun, flooding your body and your heart with high cosmic intelligence. Start to consciously breathe in this universal photonic light through your crown chakra, breathe it into your heart, and exhale it into the Light Realms as sparkling photonic light bubbles that spread out across the globe.

Continue to breathe in and out at your own pace, all the time breathing in the Universal Light and breathing it out as a gift to all life on earth. Breathe in the Cosmic Light, and breathe out the light toward all of earth's Nature Kingdoms. Send them all love from the sun.

And while you do this, observe what happens.

Now bring your attention back to the still point of your heart. See that your inner star, your inner solar star, is bright and radiant. Observe the alchemy that is happening here, with the merging of the light from Gaia and the light from the cosmos. As this alchemy intensifies, so does the Inner Light in you.

With your intention, spread this light throughout your body, to all the cells of your body, and anchor it inside of your cells, inside all of the cells of your body. Anchor this light in order to remember who you are, to remember the Being of Light that you are. In so doing, you will find an emerging confidence in your physical body. Your body is able to receive the purest light and to integrate it. Observe what all this light is doing to you.

You might feel some sensations, or you might not feel anything at all. Just trust and have faith that you are guided in the best possible way for this work.

Now observe yourself from a distance, as a radiant Being of Light. Observe the whole network of fellow travellers. See how you are all Beacons of Light. You are all Light Towers.

Now you are invited to travel to a sacred space of unity and peace in Jerusalem. Allow yourself to move easily to this portal of unity and peace. You arrive on Temple Mount, where you find yourself at the ancient Temple of Unity and Peace. It is a Golden Light Temple. At a certain time, King Salomon resided here, and it is here that he spent time with his Twin Flame, the Queen of Sheba. They are both there right now, and they invite you in. This is the holy portal of Temple Mount in Jerusalem.

Together with Mary Magdalene and Yeshua, they invite you to join a holy circle on the Temple Mount of Jerusalem. You are expected here, to prepare for tomorrow's journey. So join all the others now to make a perfect circle around the etheric Temple of Peace and Unity. In the centre of the circle stand King Salomon & the Queen of Sheba and King Yeshua & Queen Mary Magdalene. They have prepared this day for you and your fellow travellers.

Observe the beauty of this place. This portal has been here since the beginning of times. And through the light of your heart, connect with each and everyone in this network in a conscious way, heart to heart. In so doing, you make the connection even stronger. Now bring the light from your heart into the Christ grid, to nourish this grid around the earth and in the earth. With intention, bring your light into this grid, this grid of Love & Light. Bring your light to the Christ grid in the inner planes of Gaia, so that the whole light grid is fully activated. Let your light move effortlessly through the grid.

See, sense, or feel, that through the light in the Christ grid, all 144 Golden Light Temples around the earth have been activated. And observe how radiant Gaia becomes, she is a Beacon of Light in our Galaxy!

When all 144 Golden Light Temples are connected consciously, bring your attention to the network of pyramids around the globe. We know some of these pyramids, because they are visible, but most of them we have never seen because they are either under water or in the earth. Bring your light to these pyramids on Gaia, and activate your light with the highest intention. See, sense or see the pyramids as they receive your light, and the light of all your fellow travellers.

Now bring your attention back to Temple Mount in Jerusalem. From Temple Mount, connect again consciously with your heart, and from there, it is time to send a strong message of Love & Light out into the Galaxy. The message is: "IT IS DONE!" The Christ grid, the Pyramid grid, and the 144 Golden Temples are all re-connected through the human bodies of all those who have participated in restoring these structures.

Now bring your attention back to Temple Mount. See that the Eternal Flame of Peace and Unity, a Golden Flame, is getting bigger and bigger. There are many, many Ascended Masters, throughout many timelines, joining this work. There are many angelic groups joining in as well. All of the gates of Jerusalem are open. They are guarded by Angels and there are two Angels at each gate. There is a golden light emanating from outside the gates of Jerusalem, shining into the city, into the temple, into the flame. And the same golden light radiates from the Flame of Unity and Peace outward, past the gates of Jerusalem, into the world. The Light of Unity and Peace radiates all across the globe.

There is no need for you to do anything, but to simply observe it. The Flame of Unity and Peace is amplifying more and more. It is held by King Salomon & the Queen of Sheba and Yeshua & Mary Magdalene. And it is also held by you and all the others from around the globe, that hold a deep prayer of peace and unity in their hearts. There is no need for you to do anything but to be present and observe. The whole area, the whole portal of Jerusalem, is turning into gold. And it is spreading, spreading...

Now open up your heart to receive the Golden Flame of Peace and Unity. You are ready to receive the Sophia Christ Consciousness. Open up your body, your whole system, all of your awareness, to absorb this Christ Consciousness. Allow it into all of your bodies, and allow it to amplify from the inside out. Feel all the blessings and grace that are bestowed upon you. And become aware of all the Light Beings that are entering the network to support your shift in consciousness.

You are connecting to multiple circles around the globe and to many realms all around you, and together you unify in a network supporting the ascension of humanity. Connect to all the beings holding this field of Love & Light.

See, sense or feel that from within the network appears a large group of Rainbow Angels that holds the intelligence of the Twin Ray. These Angels are here to help you to heal and to raise the frequency of your chakra system. One Rainbow Angel comes to you now, to give you personal healing. Surrender to this beautiful being, who is now going to work at various levels of your energy system, your chakra system and your Rainbow Body. If you feel like doing so, you can pray for a specific healing.

Receive this healing so that you can become whole. Receive it so that you can become fully aligned with your divine blueprint. And be aware that instant healing is a real possibility in the realm of miracles.

And now invite in all souls that are ready to receive healing. Invite anyone that comes to mind. Invite anyone who needs this healing field to support his/her alignment with his/her divine blueprint and wholeness. Invite them into the network and let them be nourished by the Rainbow Angels. And while this is taking place, you can now also call in the Nature Kingdom or other beings that may be ready to receive rainbow healing. And then just simply hold space for the healing to take place.

It is now time to connect your heart to Gaia's Mineral Kingdom. The Mineral Kingdom has been strongly activated in this tremendous field of Christ Consciousness. Is there a mineral or rock that calls your attention at this time? You may have some in your home, or you may know of some in nature. Be aware that all the minerals on Gaia activate the Christ grid, each with its own unique, special radiance. So, connect to the Mineral Kingdom, and feel that deep relationship and cooperation.

When you feel you have finished all that is necessary at this moment with the Mineral Kingdom, bring your attention back to Temple Mount in Jerusalem and observe the Golden Flame of Peace and Unity, in its full radiance. See, sense, or feel how you are baptized by the liquid plasma of the Golden Flame, and by the Ascended Masters who are holding the flame. One of them comes to you, to bless you with this golden liquid plasma. Accept it with deep gratitude. It is a divine gift for all that you have done in many timelines on Gaia. It is a gift for you, because you are here now. This is a gift that comes from deep gratitude.

See and feel the gratitude of all the Ascended Masters, of the Angelic Realms and the Galactic Beings. They are so grateful that you and your fellow travellers are doing this work! They are so grateful that you heard the call and that you remembered that it was important to be here.

Feel the joy of this moment of unity with all your fellow travellers. Together, you are here to support the human, planetary and cosmic ascension.

And now take a moment to bring your highest intention into the Golden Flame of Unity and Peace. Connect for a moment with all your fellow travellers and feel how each and every one of you holds this Flame of Unity and Peace inside of you. It is this flame that dissolves anything that is untruthful. This is a flame of truth. And you can connect with this flame at any time because you now consciously hold it inside of you. You ARE the flame.

When you are ready, pay your respect to King Salomon and to the Queen of Sheba, and to King Yeshua and Queen Mary Magdalene, for guiding you today on the Temple Mount of Jerusalem. After you have thanked them, slowly return back to the centre of your heart and feel your beautiful star inside of your heart, your inner solar light that now actively holds the Flame of Unity and Peace.

While keeping your eyes closed, slowly bring your awareness to your physical body. Feel how it is, after this journey. It could be that it has changed, or it may still feel the same, but be really gentle with it. Feel your love for your body, for this beautiful vehicle that is perfect for you. Feel the sacredness of your perfect body.

And slowly start moving, just to become more aware of your physical body. Take all the time you need to fully come back. Observe your body now, with all that light you hold at the deepest levels of your physical temple. Take your time today to integrate all of this light.

Start moving your hands, your fingers, your feet and toes. Maybe you feel like moving your legs a little bit, making small movements. Move your arms, your shoulders, and your head. Maybe you might want to touch your head, to massage it a little bit. Be soft with yourself.

And whenever you're ready, but take your time, slowly open your eyes. Look around the space where you are sitting or lying. Maybe the space has changed, or maybe it is still the same. Start to fully come back with all of your awareness into this space.

Take a few deep breaths to really fill your body with oxygen. Allow your body to integrate before you start moving and be really tender and loving with yourself, today and all days.

Namaste

The Eighth Meditation: Uluru and the Rainbow Activation Code

Teachings of the Eighth Meditation

Welcome to the eighth and final meditation of this Great Passage. The ship, launched with so much courage and hope, at the beginning of the channel, has finally landed.

This final meditation was brought forth in a field of celebration and joy. It also carries with it an empowering, underlying note of resolution, commitment, and focus as we prepare ourselves for the next phase of manifesting, inside ourselves, the New Earth resonance.

This meditation was shared at the peak of the Solstice of December 21, 2020, moments before the conjunction between Saturn and Jupiter. It carries, profoundly, the frequency of that poignant and sacred time of union. The frequency offered here contains both the joy and the reverence that we feel during a marriage ceremony or the birth of a new child. It is a soul-deep joy rooted in devotion, integrity, and love.

Infused in this meditation is the profound preparation of the Aboriginal Peoples, who have prepared for this day, for 9000 years. For 9000 years, they held this solstice portal as a point of focus in their dream world. For 9000 years they have passed the knowledge of the New Earth consciousness from generation to generation, a divine inheritance of grace. They have prepared through the ages to hold the powerful energies that will shift humanity into a new, higher position on the ascending spiral.

As we come together, we join in the process of removing our heart-walls. This is the time of the Great Unveiling. This can cause some fear, as the heart-walls are what we erected to numb ourselves from feeling pain and trauma. We are learning, however, to come together in faith, and that our voice and heartfelt intentions create natural boundaries that allow us to feel safe and sovereign in our creation.

When we remove our heart walls, we gain access to previously deeply hidden wisdom and knowledge within Gaia's energetic field. The template of brotherhood and sisterhood expands. As Gaia's tribes gather together, our commitment to unity throws open the doors of the New Era. We behold ourselves anew.

The energies created by a new union are often unexpected. The New Earth is being authored by us, by our very words, by our incarnation and ability to hold light, in every given moment. We hold the blueprint, yet a blueprint can only hint at the finished manifestation. As we come together in the field of this meditation, as we come together to internally build the New Earth, we cannot predict or attach to the exact form of our creation. The new field birthed from our union will be a continuous unfolding, revealing itself to us in all of its wonder and grace.

Vitality and Health on the Earth Plane

Our Divine Mother, Gaia, offers clear guidance for moving into a state of health and vitality. Our original blueprint exists in perfect health and vitality in alignment with the earth. In the New Earth consciousness, we have transmuted the state of survival into a state of thriving. This happens as we tune into the pulse and frequency of Gaia and begin to match our own bodies and lives with her sacred rhythms. Gaia is a perfect manifestation of Source energy. When we tune into her resonance, we can easily see what is, and is not, aligned with our true nature by the effect it produces in us. When we let ourselves be drawn to that which enhances joy, love, and contentment within us, we naturally amplify joy, love, and contentment.

When you balance the Earth and Cosmic energies, resistance and fighting is not required to bring the New Earth into being. As you move through life in accordance with the natural rhythms of your united bodies, all you do and say will be naturally consecrated to healing, life-giving energies.

This meditation offers guidance for activating your Rainbow Light Body from a space of unconditional love. Once complete, you will gradually begin to embody your highest expression of self, stepping into your role as a free, sovereign creator of the New Earth. As you dwell consciously in the seat of your Light Body and in your Sacred Heart, all that you do and all that you create will naturally serve the whole. This service is the ultimate fulfilment of your soul's vow. It offers the bliss, inspiration, and joy that comes with opening to the entirety of gifts of your highest self-expression.

Uluru

Uluru is one of Gaia's chakras, and its health and purity is fundamental to the creation of peace and harmony on our planet. The Earth Guardians, who live there in a very high state of consciousness, have safeguarded this portal for eons. Uluru is considered a Divine Mother Portal of Creation where all new expressions are dreamt of and conceived. When we bring our pure light there, we contribute to the health and vitality of all life on this planet.

In this initiation we travel there to support the activation that occurred (and is still occurring) at this most significant energy centre of earth.

This meditation brings our global soul family together as one tribe to manifest the heart-dream of peace and harmony. Together we bring Heaven to Earth so that all who walk these lands can dwell in the new Garden of Eden.

As all collective energies also take place within your own personal field, this journey to Uluru will light up your own sacred centre of health and vitality. As it activates your Light Body, you will open to your power of manifesting all that you dream.

Receiving

You will notice that, even though we travel in our Light Bodies to Uluru, we will remain within the Tiny Space of the Heart. In other journeys in this Passage, you received vivid, often sensory imagery. In this journey, you will remain in a place of stillness and quiet, deep, deep within.

From the Tiny Space of the Heart you will receive the light encodings of the New Earth. These will activate new dimensions of your DNA and provide you all you need to go forth as an embodied being of the New Earth.

As the light encodings flood into your being, you are reminded that the New Earth is not something we can "achieve" but something we embody. It is, in fact, something we receive from within. Through receiving its frequencies, you will embody it, and by embodying it you will create it, naturally, effortlessly, and with great joy.

The guidance in this final meditation is to "trust yourself completely." This, ultimately, is the guidance of the New Earth. We must trust ourselves completely because, as a collective we are preparing to embark on a journey that has never been done. Together, we step off of the map. Our heart is the voice that will lead us; our soul the light that shows the way.

We invite you now to come to rest and prepare to receive the light frequencies of the New Earth.

Prepare your space.

Come to rest.

Breathe in.

And breathe out...

The Eighth Meditation and Closing Ceremony

You are invited to close your eyes, to draw a few deep breaths, and to bring your attention to the inner world of your being. Breathe in and out, slowly and gently, and with each breath, release all attachment to the outer world, just for this moment in time. Feel as all the chords to the outer world begin to dissolve and this liberates you to focus solely on your inner world. Breathe in and breathe out...

And from this space within you, connect to Mother Earth and Father Sky, in any way that feels good for you. Send them your love and gratitude for everything that you have in your life. Wait and feel how they send back their love, as they always do. They are always with you, as you are their Holy Child. You are so very precious, and they love you so much.

And now connect to all of your fellow travellers, the ones who are participating in this Great Human Passage into higher consciousness. Connect to all human beings working consciously in the light field at this time. Connect to the Light Realms: the Ascended Masters, the Angels, the Archangels, the Arcturians, and to the Pleiadians. Connect to the Animal Kingdom, the Nature Kingdom, the Mineral Kingdom and the Inner Earth Beings. Feel unity with all these realms.

Slowly bring yourself to the Sacred Space of the Heart. You know the way now. How is it in the Sacred Space of your Heart today? How does it feel today? Observe this in all of the cells of your body. If the light has not been turned on in the Sacred Heart Space, simply allow it to turn itself on now.

There may be images that are important for you at this time. Or perhaps presences that are important for you, with messages or special guidance. Just stay open. Allow the mind to be completely quiet. Just stay here for a few minutes, listen and observe.

And now, from the Sacred Space of the Heart, drop into the Tiny Space of the Heart. This is the Universal Heart, the point of all Creation.

Just say to yourself with intention, "I am going to move into the Tiny Space of the Heart, into the inner toroidal field." You can move there any way you want. It makes absolutely no difference. It may look various ways when you get there. You may end up in a cave, or in the stars. It may be dark, even though it is filled with light. Allow yourself to settle into the stillness of this place. You will feel absolute tranquillity. Sink deeply into this peacefulness.

When you have become completely still, allow the light to come into your field of vision. And if you are still moving, keep going until you feel yourself stopping. Once you arrive in this place of complete stillness, follow your intuition about what it is that you ought to do. Trust yourself completely. This is the space from which all is created.

Reside in this tranquil state for a few minutes.

And from this space, ask the Golden Sophia Christ Light, the Holy Spirit, to come and completely dissolve all suffering on Gaia. And in the stillness of the Tiny Space of the Heart, allow it to happen. Everything is possible from this space of creation, from the absolute peace of this most holy place.

And now connect to all of the tribes across the planet. Reconnect with all the races, all of the cultures, and all of the ancient tribes. Watch through the Christ grid how all of the last protection mechanisms dissolve from the hearts of those prepared to connect fully with the Christ grid. The veils that have been protecting all the ancient knowledge, all the ancient wisdom, are now ready to dissolve. Now this ancient knowledge and wisdom will be freely available to all who are in the space of unconditional love and who are connected to the Christ grid. This is the Great Unveiling.

All of this knowledge, wisdom and solidarity, this brotherhood and sisterhood, now expands freely across the Earth. This is the gathering of the tribes, and together, in unity, we are unstoppable. Feel this network of Oneness. And feel how all the pieces are coming together. And see, sense or feel how you are connected to the One Heart.

And through this field of the One Heart, you will travel now, with others in the Great Passage, to Uluru, Australia.

When you arrive in this most sacred portal, the one whose purity creates vitality and health on our earth plane, you will see, sense, or feel the elders and the community that is gathered there today. Honour and bow to the aboriginal people who are leading the ceremony. We will make a circle around them, to support them, to protect them, and to strengthen them. Feel yourself there. See yourself there in this great rite of Passage for humanity. Open your heart fully, with the knowledge that you are an essential part of the human tribe.

Feel the field of the One Heart, pulsating through all who are present. This Tribe of the One Heart will send the most beautiful, Divine Love to Mother Earth, to the heart of Mother Earth. This love will revitalize her and give her energy. It will sustain her with this flow of love and gratitude.

See how the field becomes more and more full of light. She is your Mother, she gives you everything you have here on earth, absolutely everything. Amplify this field of love for, and gratitude to, this divine being who is so generous and beautiful. Give her more and more love, so she can move into her next phase of evolution. So she can ascend and so you can ascend with her; so she can heal, and so that you can heal.

Observe how this energy amplifies and moves throughout Gaia. Just hold space for this to happen. Witness this great field of Love & Light. Mark this moment of renewal for all life on this planet.

Become conscious of all of the Light Beings that are here supporting this process. The Pleiadians, the Arcturians, the Ascended Masters, the vast realms of angelic beings, beings from Inner Earth, and so many others are supporting this moment of renewal, the renewal of Gaia and humanity.

As the energies continue to activate and move, your DNA is turned on at a whole new level. This is directed by your Higher Self, and has been time-coded for this moment in time. Just allow that to happen on its own, within this great field of Love & Light. This light moves through your whole system – the physical, emotional and mental bodies. Just allow it to happen all on its own. Let it move where it needs to move at this moment in time.

This is a rainbow activation, and you may see all the colours of the rainbow moving through your system. This activation is moving you to the next level of your potential as a Human Creator Being on Gaia. Allow these colours to activate your system, and to move deep into your DNA and into the atomic structure of your body.

See, sense or feel how these frequencies are moving through the whole human tribe, through the entire human family. See, sense or feel how these frequencies are moving through Gaia, and how we are evolving as a unified pattern, all together.

See how these frequencies are moving out through the ley lines of the earth, bringing new information, new ways of being and perceiving, new consciousness, new ways of caring for the planet, new ways of living together, new systems, and new informational codes. We can feel all the ley-lines activating, everywhere on Gaia, with this new information.

Continue to hold space for this activation, for this leap of light, for this quantum leap in consciousness. And as this process continues, and will continue over the next period of time, keep it with you in your heart, in your consciousness.

And now bring yourself back to the Tiny Space of the Heart. Bring your awareness back to the Tiny Space of the Heart, and to the stillness of this space. And from the stillness of the space, become aware of the channel of light that was opened in the opening ceremony, with all of our brothers and sisters from across the surface of the earth, from the Inner Earth, and from across the Galaxy.

It is now time to thank all of the beings that have been with us in this Great Passage.

Thank the seven directions.

Thank the five elements.

Thank Mary Magdalene and Yeshua, who overlit this Great Passage.

Thank Grandmother Anna and the Holy Family.

Thank the Divine Mother Sophia of all Creation.

Thank Archangel Metatron and Archangel Michael.

Thank Lord Melchizedek and the Melchizedek Beings, the Arcturians and the Pleiadians.

Thank the Realms of the Archangels and the Angels – all of the Angelic Realms that have supported this process.

Thank the Council of Whale Elders and the Lemurian High Council.

Thank the Light Beings from the Inner Earth.

Thank all the Ascended Masters that help, support, and guide humanity.

Thank the Circle of Crystal Skulls, the thirteen crystal skulls.

Thank the Galactic Federation of Light.

Thank Lord Ganesh, Merlin, Babaji, the Waitaha, Saint Germain and Pallas Athena.

Thank the Beings from the Waters, the Elemental Beings, the Plant Kingdom, the Animal Kingdom and the Mineral Kingdom.

And now thank all of the Guides and Angels that you called in during the opening ceremony.

Thank all the forces of protection that have made this work fluid and smooth, and all those who have kept the field of unity, love and light so that this work could take place.

Please give deep, heartfelt thanks to all those who are in this Great Passage with you at this time on Gaia.

And slowly, bring your attention back to your body. Take a few deep breaths, gently bringing your awareness back to the space you are in. Slowly start to bring your attention to your fingers and your toes, and wiggle these a little, in order to feel your physical temple. Slowly begin to stretch, or massage your shoulders, arms and legs, all the time keeping your eyes closed and maintaining an inner silence.

Take a few more slow breaths, and when you are ready, slowly open your eyes. You have arrived back in this paradise called Gaia.

Namaste

As your heart's light

Merges with that of the Earth and Sun,

You will feel yourself becoming

A beacon of light for the New Earth.

Arrival

Welcome to the far bank of the river. You have arrived! Take a moment to feel yourself, cloaked now in the ineffable rainbow light of your Higher Self.

As you turn from the river to the next phase in your journey, you will see, stretching before you, the vast beyond of your life. The path you are about to step on will lead you in ever increasing spirals, to the heart of your purpose in this lifetime. Your Illuminated Heart and the Light Body you now consciously inhabit are your greatest resources in these unknown lands. When you are on unfamiliar ground, or when you feel you have lost your way, your Divine Heart and Light Body will shine forth, bringing to you all of the resources and guidance that you need. You stand on Gaia as a Christed Being, a beacon to all of those who are lost in the darkness. Embrace the divine power that comes from beyond you and from within you. It is your destiny.

You will come to know anew this integrated, illuminated body. It will speak to you of what it needs. You will learn to balance ritual and spontaneity as, especially in these early phases of integration, it may ask for unexpected things at unexpected times. Let your body expand and contract with each breath, flowing and taking shape as needed for its healing, integration, and ultimate flourishing. Let go, now, of thinking how it "should" look, feel, or behave, and trust that in all moments, even those that are difficult, it is fully in control, unfolding perfectly with the larger, unseen plan.

For your physical body, sleep, take time out to observe, rest, and provide yourself with healthy, nourishing food. Take time in nature to ground yourself as a response to the light that is coming in. Your physical body is your personal temple for life on Gaia. It requires respect, care, and love. Give yourself what you need and trust that the time and resources will be available. Trust, also, that the world and those around you will sort themselves out while you care for yourself. This is a sacred time for you to be with yourself and your body, discovering your natural rhythms and your real needs.

For your emotional body, seek out, without apology, the people, places, and contexts that are nourishing to you. This is not simply important at this time but it is truly a necessity. Remember that your life, your presence, and your attention are sacred. Take care about who you share yourself with. Like the honeybee, let yourself be drawn to the people, things, and activities that nourish you and leave you feeling filled-up and loved. Your discernment, precision, and willingness to begin drawing healthy boundaries at this time is the beginning of your Divine Masculine activation, that which will carry you forward into the next phase of our journey together: The Twin Ray Oneness Consciousness.

For your mental body, seek out information that comes from pure sources and which awakens your conscious understanding. Find books, films or teachings that calm the mind and expand your horizons. As much as possible, detach from any information or source that seeks to seed and spread fear. Let your wonderful mind be calmed and expanded by the Voice of the Divine in all of its forms. As you open to this intention, more and more resources and information that support your divine purpose will flow to you.

For your soul, allow yourself time to reside often in the Sacred Space of the Heart, for integration and contemplation. Repeat the meditations, as you feel called, for ongoing alchemical integration. Ask (always!) for support and guidance from your guides! They are here for you as much as we are.

Lastly, we want you to know how grateful we are that you joined us in this Great Passage. We are not remote authors, but human beings who can feel your presence as loved – and loving – soul family. We are so grateful that you joined us. In the times ahead, know that we, and our whole community, are here for you. You can connect with us in the Light Realms or through the inner planes. If you need practical, earthly support for your process,

174

from other beings who are deeply familiar with the work, you can join us through our community at Mary Magdalene's School.

We also encourage you to take time to celebrate your courage and light! This is the beginning of a wondrous new journey. Know that your purpose and power as a being on this planet will continue to unfold. All is well and all is perfectly orchestrated in space and time.

Welcome Traveller. Welcome Home!

Postface
by Anna & Petra

Mary Magdalene's Great Passage online gathering concluded on 21.12.2020. This very important turning point for consciousness on Gaia heralded the beginning of a whole new epoch of life on this planet, requiring a tremendous, accelerated transformation of consciousness at an individual and collective level.

After the intense journey of eight global meetings over a period of three weeks, we were ready to rest and enjoy the Christmas period with our families. However, only two days later, both of us heard a knocking on the door, so-to-speak, from the higher realms, and our visitors entered...

Though we were in two different countries and not in daily communication, King Solomon came into our fields in two very different ways, giving us each so much information and so many impulses that on the seventh day, despite our need for a holiday, we dived into the field together again to understand what it was that was needed from us. King Solomon and the Queen of Sheba were there, waiting. They asked us to continue the global work, to keep the focus, and to bring people together to bring in the Light. We understood that there are many descendants from the line of Solomon and that this lineage needed to be activated in a strong way at this time.

The consciousness held in the House of David in the masculine line and the consciousness of the female House of Magdala needed to come together in a deeper way, to anchor new levels of sacred consciousness into the planetary grid. An invitation arose in our alignment with them to work on specific layers in the Sacred Temple of Salomon, and to inaugurate the Era of the Twin Ray Oneness Consciousness, which would lay the foundation for a New Earth civilization based on unity consciousness.

We hope you will join us for a continuation of this spectacular journey through consciousness! We are so grateful to be on this Earth Walk together! May you all be blessed and reside in the field of unconditional love.

Together we hold and quicken

The Universal Light on Golden Gaia

To support the anchoring of

The Sophia Christ Light on Earth.

The Great Passage:
Journey into the New Earth

This is the first book to be published by Libraries of Light Media & Publishing. Through the careful guidance of Mary Magdalene, it holds the power of prophecy and alchemy that is the essence of the Magdalene force. This book is one of the ways we are creating a template, a reality structure for the emergence of the feminine dynamic of the Christ presence in the era to come. The concepts within are anchored in the archetypal structures of the mysteries, the sacred powers, and that which has already been established through mystical revelation.

At this time in history and herstory, we are no longer writing on the fringes of mysticism. This book, like our other projects, engages the quantum energy, the source of the Divine Force, through vortexes, spirals and portals in the centre of the light, in the very centre of the light of the Feminine Christ Force.

As mentioned, on December 21st, 2020, Gaia entered the Aquarian age in a whole new way – a time prophesied for all of humanity to come together in unity consciousness. The prophecies for this time speak of the feminine energy rising and coming into harmony with the sacred masculine. This is a time in which humanity steps into a higher evolutionary framework and begins to live and act as One on Gaia. It is a time when the human family is making a breath-taking, quantum leap up the evolutionary spiral.

This book provides experiential and practical tools for embodying the energies, frequencies, and encodings of the New Earth.

Mary Magdalene's Great Passage: Journey into the New Earth offers a process for activating our Light Bodies. The meditations support us in re-membering our immaculate state, which is our pure divinity. They bring us into resonance with this immaculate state that already exists. Together, from our connection with the Divine Mother, we explore the infinite power, compassion, and wisdom of our sovereign ability to create new worlds from the Sacred Space of the Heart. With the final meditation, we use our skills of heart-creation to activate at higher levels our Light Body. This Light Body enables us to have a personal connection to, and knowledge of, the whole universe. It is an essential part of our energy anatomy, allowing us to access various spiritual technologies that will be necessary for living in the New Earth.

Each book glimmers with hidden secrets,

Beckoning you to touch, to sense,

To absorb its radiance.

They glow like seeds,

Each with its own unique Christed Light,

Perfect time-capsules holding the energy

Of our collective Passage.

Guides and Ascended Masters of this Passage

Mother Earth

Father Sky

Mary Magdalene

Yeshua

Grandmother Anna

Mother Mary

The Family Line of David

Archangel Metatron

Lord Melchizedek and the Melchizedek Beings

The Arcturians

The Pleiadeans

The Council of Whales Elders

The Lemurian High Council

All Lemurian & Light Beings from Inner Earth, Agartha, and Telos

The Brotherhood of the Light

Traveller and the 13 Crystal Skulls

Galactic Federation of Light

Archangel Michael and his army

The Angelic Realms

Antharion

Babaji

Earth Kingdoms: the Animal Kingdom, the Plant Kingdom, the Mineral Kingdom, and the Elemental Kingdom

Kwan Yin

The Divine Mother (in all of her infinite manifestations)

The Hathors

The Creator Sophia

Lady Nada

Pallas Athena

Lady Portia

Lady Venus

The Board of the Divine Feminine

The Great Central Sun

El Morya

Holy Spirit Shekinah

Lord Maitreya

Saint Germain

Paul the Venetian

King Solomon

The Queen of Sheba

The Rainbow Angels

Glossary

A glossary can be found on Mary Magdalene's School website: https://marymagdaleneschool.com/the-glossary

Who We Are

As we introduce ourselves, we would like to acknowledge that this book was not created by us individually, per se, but by the cosmic Feminine Christ Consciousness that has blessed us with the visions, talents, resources, and training to receive and relay the information contained herein. Mary Magdalene tirelessly aligned us with the highest divine potential of this journey. We have become instruments of this divine intention for the manifestation of a whole new energy system, which is a Holy Grail.

We have been asked to pioneer human consciousness, by stepping into her source of illumination and mystical power. This experience is life changing, because we are not working on the peripheral fringes of mysticism. We have entered a state of consciousness through which we engage directly with the quantum energy field, the source of the divine force that exists in the vortex and portals at the centre of the Light. And we are the guardians of the purity of that which is given life through the womb of the Divine Feminine. We are guardians of this sacred gift. We walk this path of service in deep humility to the Cosmic Forces of Nature.

We would like to acknowledge that this book was a collective effort and could not have been possible without all of the individuals named in the "gratitude" section, and many, many more besides.

The details we share in this section are facts that are most pertinent to the transmission of this book.

Petra Maria Brussen

Born in The Netherlands, Petra was gifted with a strong connection to, and understanding of, the subtle realms; Petra knows the invisible world as some know the visible.

Petra is truly a Being of Light. She carries an ancient lineage that evokes the solar force. For many lifetimes she has trained as a priestess in the Solar Temples, enacting and presiding over ceremonies and rituals in places around the globe and Inner Earth. Petra is a living embodiment of the Solar Sophia.

This manifests in her being as palpable warmth of spirit, unfailing graciousness, and a deep love for all of humanity. Regardless of her context – whether challenging or easeful – Petra shines as a living sun for all who know her, with irrepressible warmth, humour, and compassion. She uses her powers of solar illumination and innate generosity of heart to mirror the highest divinity of everyone she meets. This is evident in her personal relationships and her professional endeavors.

She is guided, awakened by, and embodies the presence of Mary Magdalene. She incarnates pre-Lemurian consciousness and teaches this knowledge, inviting humanity to step to a new level of earth life anchored in inner and outer peace, harmony and Oneness. In the year 2000, Petra and her twin soul Ton founded a school, *NostraSofia*, in which consciousness work was the basis for creating the New Era. The life and death of her twin soul awakened her to the realm of Divine Oneness and to her purpose in life. It is her heart's deepest wish to lead humanity back into the Unified Field, and to help humans remember their divine powers through the consciousness of the White-Gold Ray.

Petra has a deep wisdom connected to Gaia, to the visible and invisible worlds of the Animal, Plant, and Mineral Kingdoms. As a myrrhophore, she creates *Xrysma Anointing Oils*, sacred oils that serve as ascension tools.

Aside from her Business and Marketing degrees, Petra has studied Nature Medicine, Phytotherapy, Etheric Oils, Jungian Psychology,

Astrology, Reiki, Reflexology, and Energetic Healing. She has also undergone training and initiations through several Mystery Schools and *Trinfinity Academy*, and has participated in workshops such *as Drunvalo Melchizedek's* Awakening of the Illuminated Heart. For over 25 years, as a "Hearts Leader", she led business organizations and projects from the heart. All of this experience is integrated in her co-founding of Mary Magdalene's School with Anna Vanickova, which allows her to stay at the forefront of human consciousness. She now lives both in the Netherlands and in France (Vézelay).

Anna Vanickova

Passionate, vibrant, curious, and keenly intellectual, Anna's formidable combination of compassion and acumen has the power to penetrate even the most intimidating obscurity, lifting up the seed of light, truth, and integrity from the darkest of places. Anna is an anointed soul who received the Eucharist at the hands of Mary Magdalene. The Eucharist, traditionally an initiation uniting Matter and Spirit, in this case was not an initiation so much as a confirmation of Anna's already-realized understanding of the nature of Heaven and Earth. This communion, through Anna, actually gave birth to a new understanding in the Light Realms of the sacred union between Form and Formless. As such, she is able to live in both realms at once. In this way, Anna is truly a Rainbow Bridge, comfortable traversing the path between Form and Formless, Matter and Spirit, God and Body.

This stillpoint between the two realms, for Anna, is a thread that connects her many lifetimes and has allowed her to midwife new creations into the material world. Her soul has training as a spiritual midwife, and through many lifetimes of witnessing and stewarding new life into the world, Anna's role in this lifetime is as an accoucheuse for the New Earth.

Anna's life leading up to this point has been richly adorned by her diverse interests, among them a love for children, a passion for spiritual study and healing, and a constant search for truth. She is a devoted mother and wife, bringing dignity and power to these roles.

A born visionary, teacher, healer, and community-builder, Anna worked in her early years as a pianist and multi-disciplinary artist in Canada, her birth country. Upon moving to Prague in 1990, she joined the post-1989 spiritual revolution of Eastern Europe. With the support of many spiritual masters, she began to remember her healing and teaching abilities, working with multidimensional, intergalactic awareness, Ascended Masters, Angels, Dragons and many other Galactic and Inner Earth Light Beings.

Over her lifetime she received training in, and has practiced, various healing modalities – One Brain Kinesiology, Body Code, Reiki, Reconnective Healing, Healing with Christ Energies, Shamanic work, and Sound Healing. She has also received many initiations by Sri Kaleshwar and through the inner realms by the Order of Melchizedek, the Arcturians, the Guardians of the Sacred Flames, as well as in many Inner Earth temples.

In Prague, she co-founded and guided many community projects, such as the Library for Women's Wisdom, The MA Women's Circle, the Spiritual Women's Circle 11 Taras, and the Forest School Zeme ZeMe. In 2002 she co-founded the NGO Prameni o.p.s, dedicated to promoting human potential through the Arts, Education and Spirituality. At the present time she lives in Vézelay, France, where she is on the board of a regional healer's association. Her vision is to reconnect people with their Divine Light and with the deepest desires of their Sacred Hearts, the realm of Miracle Consciousness. She is, with Petra Van der Linden-Brussen, co-founder of Mary Magdalene's School, which allows her to stay at the forefront of consciousness.

Katherine Newburgh, Ph.D

This book was scribed by Katherine Newburgh (Kate). The role of scribe is paradoxical in that it seems to hold many opposites within it. The role of "scribe" is at once independent and collaborative, personal and public, didactic and intuitive, practical and artistic, responsive and creative. The scribe translates holy scripture from the higher realms and, in so doing, shapes channels of ascension. The scribe is the keeper of the written word, and words are the very mechanism of creation. The scribe must be steadfast, perceptive, and immune to compromise, as it is the voice of the book, and not the fleeting preferences of the ego, that she has committed to bringing forward. Through listening to the needs of the book, the scribe learns to stand in her own power even as she consecrates it to a higher purpose.

Kate has found that "scribe" must be committed to as a life's work. The role itself requires that these books be birthed through the totality and shaped by her unique shamanic voice. Thus, the writing process for this book has demanded a relentless commitment to purity and solitude in order for her to remain in resonance with the frequency of the information coming through. She has spent much time in communication with the book itself, withdrawn from the outside world.

Kate is honoured to be the scribe for this book. She was drawn to Mary Magdalene's School at the very beginning of The Great Passage in November, 2020. She had just left all she had known and begun a new cycle in her life. This cycle turned out to be a final push in shaking off the trappings of a world (and worldview) defined by limitations.

She internalized the meditations of this book, first on a farm in Colorado, and then in solitude in the rainforest in Puerto Rico where she had taken herself on a writing retreat. She emerged from the process transformed and ready to share the power of this work with others in the best way she knew how – by writing.

Kate has always been a writer and she completed her first book at age six. It was entitled, The *Vegetarian Cat*, which even then betokened a precocious sense of irony and, perhaps more palpably, a love of cats. However, it took her until age 36 to fully embrace writing as her deepest calling and gift in life.

A combination of mainly Earth and Air, Kate has always been drawn to the challenge of making visible the unseen realms of existence. She has a unique ability to live on both planes at once, and has spent her life translating the intangible dynamics of higher realms into clear and practical understandings. She has honed this skill throughout her life, including in the field of academia. As a researcher, her most notable peer-reviewed article holds the subtitle "Mapping the Ineffable."

Her work as scribe for this book has helped deepen her process of re-membering. While continuing to write her own works, she has been grateful for the opportunity to make visible and concrete the magic of these guided teachings and meditations. The scribing of this book, which required a full-body, full-life immersion into Mary Magdalene's energy field (including moving, for a time, to Vézelay, France) has heralded new and completely unexpected gifts in her life. Her wish and intention is for the readers of this book to experience the same life-giving magic that she felt when first entering the field with Anna and Petra.

Testimonies about Meditations from Mary Magdalene's School

The initiatic meditations of Mary Magdalene's School are internationally renowned for their beauty and power of transformation. They are transmitted during Global Online Gatherings, Global Meditations and in the Re-Membership Program.

Here are a few comments from participants of these meditational journeys:

Extraordinary beautiful and full of wisdom, both of you!! I experience the most beautiful inner journeys thanks to you calm voices and guidance... So grateful to join you for more than a year and feeling so blessed! Your meditations are the treasures in my life and inner being! Thank you both from the bottom of my heart and Soul! Marie Jose Soons

Thank you so much for doing what you are doing to transform our world into the beautiful, wonderful place that it is meant to be. I am really grateful to participate in these meditations that unify people from all over the world and are so helpful in this time of Transition. Thank You... Thank You... Thank You! Anneke Lek

Thank you for all the work you are doing, for all the opportunities you are providing and for holding space for everybody. The meditations are profound and beyond my understanding. So much happens and I can't recollect it, it happens in another realm or consciousness. I feel words cannot express enough my gratitude. I look forward to grow in every aspect possible, because your work is bringing me to the next level. In deep gratitude, Maartje Groeneveld

When I entered my heart space I landed in the palm of a giant hand, God's hand which was showing me that I was completely safe and supported. Thank you to both of you for your incredible work. Yolande Sylvain

So very grateful for your gifts of guidance, love and transformation. Kathy Connors

Thank you so much, such powerful energy, but at the same time such stillness, such love and gratitude. Graca Cruz

And I bow to you dear Petra and Anna! This gathering was so profound and of a depth I could not have imagined before this Journey started. Rian

So full of love and compassion, Petra & Anna led us through our own process, with their outstanding knowledge and connection to the world of love & the heart! Judith Bootsman

Since "discovery" of this Mary Magdalene School my mind has been stretched more in the past year than ever before. I have discovered worlds and beings that I'd never even thought actually existed. And some beyond even my imagination. This is on a whole other level. Anika Lewis

I am really grateful to Anna and Petra. Thank you for changing my life. Tanvi Gaur

The experience in my heart was beyond my imagination. Harma Musschenga

I'm still flabbergasted. And still on the bed where I listened to the meditation... SuurMaj

View the complete archive of meditations from Mary Magdalene's School: https://marymagdaleneschool.com/meditations/

How to find us at
Mary Magdalene's School

If you would like to stay connected to, or learn more about the work of, Mary Magdalene's School, please subscribe to our newsletter via our website:

www.marymagdaleneschool.com

You can also find us on the following platforms
FACEBOOK: http://www.facebook.com/marymagdaleneschool
INSTAGRAM: Mary Magdalene School instagram
YOUTUBE: Mary Magdalene School
TELEGRAM: Mary Magdalene School (push the "join" button)

Re-membership Program
Mary Magdalene's School has a membership program, called the Re-membership Program. This program takes the form of a private group in Mary Magdalene's School, with regular meetings on ZOOM and FB, in which soul-family can participate, interact regularly with Petra and Anna and other members, and receive support. This is a community in which like-minded people gather and different activities are facilitated throughout the year. These activities are always offered in line with the creation of the New Earth and respond to the calling of the present moment.

More information: http://marymagdaleneschool.com/mary-magdalenes-re-membership/

We can also be contacted by email:
info@marymagdaleneschool.com

Libraries of Light

Libraries of Light Media & Publishing is an initiative of Mary Magdalene's School. This publishing section has organically developed under Mary Magdalene's guidance to share teachings she finds important for humanity at this time. She is opening our consciousness to the records of the Libraries of Light so that they can be re-introduced into the world in a whole new way, aligned with the times in which we are living. We are in a deep state of humility and gratitude as we co-create this book with Mary Magdalene's guidance.

Libraries of Light
Media & Publishing

Photograph: Statue of Mary Magdalene in the
Basilique Sainte Marie Madeleine de Vézelay.

Printed in Great Britain
by Amazon

42624795R00109